PRAISE FOR
All Roads Lead to Dockweiler

"Rick Bickerstaff's book seamlessly weaves together the spiritual depth of devotionals with the exhilarating world of surf stories. As someone who appreciates the sentiment behind 'Pray for Surf,' I found this book to be not only a great read but also a meaningful journey. Just as we pray for waves, may this book inspire us to pray for more faith, more courage, and more meaningful connections with the divine as we navigate the waves of life. Remember, Jesus was a surfer too, but He walked the waves without a board, showing us the ultimate example of grace and courage."

—Israel Campbell, Pastor and Author of *The Art of Sonship*

All Roads Lead to Dockweiler blends Rick's two core passions; surfing and spirituality. It is filled with entertaining stories of Rick's own adventures as well as super practical tips for any Angeleno navigating the local surfing scene, including how to avoid parking tickets!

—Jon Ritner, Author of *Positively Irritating: Embracing a Post-Christian World to Form a More Faithful and Innovative Church*

"A keen, precise, and always insightful meditation on surfing, faith and, actually life itself, with all its highs and lows and good days and bad. If you know the surf world in Southern California, this book is for you, and if you don't and want to learn, this book is an especially important primer on what to do and where to go. Oh, and hey, there's even a little skiing and skateboarding too. *All Roads Lead to Dockweiler* is a terrific guide to living on many levels."

—Jason Pomerance, Author of *Celia At 39* and Los Angeles surfer

"Bickerstaff's refreshing and intimate Angeleno chronicles captures a specific moment in time. I truly enjoyed this meditation on growth, artistry, and young adulthood. And I have a newfound appreciation for my favorite intersection of Sunset Blvd. at Sunrise."

—Jennica Schwartzman, Author, Actor and Film Producer

ALL ROADS LEAD TO DOCKWEILER

Devotions from the Ocean in the City of Angels

by

Rick Bickerstaff

 HIGH DIVE
PUBLISHING

Published by
www.HighDivePublishing.com
HighDivePublishing@gmail.com
Twitter/X @HighDivePublish
Instagram @HighDivePublishing

Cover illustration by Andrew Bartleson
Book design by Megan Katsanevakis

THANK YOU SO MUCH for purchasing *All Roads Lead to Dockweiler: Devotions from the Ocean in the City of Angels*! Included with your book purchase is a digital download of the accompanying album *Golden Coast Summertime* by my alt-folk project Yonder Breaks!

It was always my dream to release music alongside written content, so it feels very special to be able to share these songs with you. As your read the book, you will find lyrics printed at various points that complement the material. When that happens, please make sure to listen to the appropriate song so you can get the full multimedia experience! Of course, the album is also meant to be listened to on its own, which I hope you will also do!

This QR code will allow you to download the album in its entirety. Thank you for joining me on this journey and I hope you enjoy both *All Roads Lead to Dockweiler* as well as *Golden Coast Summertime*!

—Rick

TABLE OF CONTENTS

FOREWORD

by Peter L. Harmon

I MET RICK IN the spring of 2008 when we were randomly placed as roommates at a semester long film program in Los Angeles. We bonded over the classic film *Three Ninjas* and our shared love of writing and making movies. He introduced me to the band Copeland, for which I am eternally grateful, and he opened my mind to the concept of mixing more than one kind of cereal together to create Dr. Frankenstein's Breakfast Bowl.

During our time in that program we had many long talks, late night discussions, and conversations over $5 Little Caesars' large pizzas. We didn't have much money but we had a lot of ambition, and Hollywood dreams. I learned that Rick is a deep thinker, even though he is sometimes slow to speak in his deep voiced, trademark Southern drawl, mixed with SoCal surfer lingo. I may have known more about indie films at the time, but he was a student of Jesus' teachings in a way that I wasn't. He read his Bible while I read some tattered copy of an old Stephen King novel. He listened to praise songs in addition to the early 2000s emo we both enjoyed. I learned more from him that semester than that if you mixed Count Chocula with Reese's Puffs that you created a soupy, peanutbuttery and chocolately breakfast dessert dream.

In our decade plus friendship I have counted Rick as someone to look to for advice, to read my various writing projects, and as a constant collaborator. We've written screenplays together, shot a web series, created comedy sketches, and even acted in our friend Taylor's various viral videos. He is a talented musician as well as writer.

So when he told me he had written a book that was a combination of a memoir, surfing tutorial, and devotional... and oh yeah there's an album that goes with it, I didn't balk at the chance to check it out, despite not having much interest in surfing and usually preferring the aforementioned fictional King stories to nonfiction. My first read of the book was emotional, as I had recently traversed the contiguous United States and bought a house on the East Coast, after living in Los Angeles for 14 years. And I totally relate to the nostalgic and emotional connection you can have to a location, as Rick outlines in the following book with his fond memories of a specific Pacific surf spot. I have the community pool I grew up going to that I have written about in a young adult book series called *The Happenstances...*, Max Fischer had his Rushmore, and Rick has Dockweiler.

So I invite you to read the following written words, which in their sum create a unique and engaging book. There is depth and emotion... and logistics about where to park if you're visiting a certain beach. There are lessons that relate to everyday life. There is a love for a city and its surrounding natural beauty. There is appreciation for God's gifts, however they show up. And overwhelmingly there is a sense of love, joy, peace, and enough of the other fruits of the Spirit to fill a cup from a Los Angeles fruit cart.

PROLOGUE

Sunrise at Sunset

SUNRISE AT SUNSET. SOUNDS nice, doesn't it? Also, impossible. But not in Los Angeles, California, where Sunset Boulevard intersects the Pacific Coast Highway at what is a sleek, long right-handed point break (where a wave breaks at a specific spot and travels alongside the shore, rather than breaking straight into the shore). It's a skate ramp of a wave that is easy to ride, and catchable at two glorious points: One for the in-shape surfers who can make the paddle, and then one for everyone else. (Guess which category I belonged to...) My friend Mitchel and I had been trying to organize a sunrise trip there for months, but the timing never seemed to work out. Eventually, there came the day when I would leave Los Angeles and relocate to Charleston, South Carolina – where I am originally from – so I was running out of time to make this happen. And so, with only a couple of weekends left, we finally put this magic moment of surfing together.

I packed up my 2005 Subaru Baja – a Frankenstein of a car if there ever was one; half truck, half four-door sedan (it was turbo charged though, which earned me some cool points) – at 5:30AM and headed out to pick up Mitchel and his wife Rochelle. Our friend Justin was going to meet us there, as well as Tyler; a stellar crew for the epic "sunrise at sunset" session we had been talking about for months. The drive was easy as the early morning haze that frequents the West Coast added a dimension to the air I knew I was going to miss. If you have ever traveled on the Pacific Coast Highway (also known as the PCH), you know it is one of the most beautiful drives in the United States; even if you haven't seen the rest of the country, its ranking is inherent as you glide along the subtle curves that follow the coast. Heading north from Los Angeles, you begin to exit the bustle of Santa Monica just as the mountains grow like the heads of giants in front of you. It is amazing how so much of the West Coast goes from beach to a sharp incline in only a few hundred yards, but this is one of the things that makes California magical.

The waves in this stretch of Santa Monica tend to be flat beach breaks (breaking directly onto the sand, as opposed to the aforementioned point break) and are generally less accessible than the waves before or after it. However, driving this part gives you a good idea of what you're heading into: if it's flat, start praying. If it's big and slamming down on the beach like an unrideable concrete drainage pipe, get ready for a great session. Just keep your eye on the road because it is perpetually under construction…

On this particular day, it looked more like a lake than the furious Pacific Ocean. We asked each other if anyone looked at the surf report: "Nope," was the sheepish consensus. These days there is little excuse for enduring a bad session unknowingly. Surfline and its extensive network of webcams ensures most of the world's surf breaks can be seen from anywhere with a phone or computer; not to mention local surf reports, cameras planted on beachside restaurants with free access and some other websites that Mitchel likes to use that often go out of business after a few short years. I remember in my younger days when we would call the local surf shop's surf report phone number. On a typical Saturday or Sunday, there were so many inquiring surfers you usually had to call about six or seven times before you got through. If the man on the other end had left a favorable recording, off you were. Otherwise, it would become a yard-work day, or maybe you would settle for skateboarding, if it wasn't too hot in Charleston (which it usually was).

I always thought it would have been fun to be the local Folly Beacher who got to ride his oversized, rusty beach cruiser down to the grass-laden shore every morning at 5:00AM, checking the waves and informing the city about its likelihood of catching a good one. It was an honorable position; thankless, but important, like the watchtower guard of an old medieval village. "Waves abound!" he would yell to the townsfolk with triumph in his shouts, and then go back to the surf shop to man the counter while the rest of the world tanned away the day. A martyr for the masses. These were the heroes of old, that have now been replaced by the cold wires and lenses of webcams and technology.

Anyway…we congregated at the spot: Sunset and PCH. There is a Taco Bell that I have visited way too many times (but still somehow, not enough), which, if heading south from Malibu, is always a good stop right before you get into LA proper with its high-priced pubs and bistros. There is also a grocery store and a gas station; kind of an all-around fill-up before you head into Malibu in search of bigger surf and a better life.

There we were, fulfilling our dreams of said life, parked nearly illegally on the side of the road that would soon become convoluted with beach-goers brave enough to endure Malibu traffic. It was fairly peaceful, the way the water lapped against the rocks at the peak of the point, but I think all of us would have traded that calm morning for the roar of head-high waves peeling like a light blue banana along the shore. Eventually, we decided that this epic session was a bust, and so after taking a few pictures, we headed to Topanga where the surf report (we finally checked it) promised at least a little more height.

Mitchel contemplating the lake that Sunset and PCH had become.
(Photo by author)

There certainly were more waves to surf, and everyone else who had gotten up that early to paddle out knew it: about thirty guys populated the break, competing for one-to-two-foot waves in a desperate effort to justify their choice to surf instead of sleep. Not one to compete for small surf, I voted we head back to town, where the swell seemed to be producing something a little more rideable. With some convincing, the rest of the crew agreed, and so, after watching the sun rise over the Santa Monica hills for the last time, we backtracked, past Sunset Boulevard, around Taco Bell and through

Santa Monica, down the 405 freeway, all the way to LAX where we hung a soft right onto the 105 freeway. This bumpy road in disrepair dumps right into the beach, to a place where I had had more magical moments than all of La La Land put together; my favorite place to enjoy the coast in Los Angeles county: Dockweiler State Beach.

All roads lead to Dockweiler, I thought as we headed west, and today it felt true, as our search for surf ended up in a place I had known to be moderately reliable. If you've never heard of Dockweiler, congratulations, you are amongst the greater population of the world. Even the world of surfers. Even the world of surfers in Los Angeles! No one surfs Dockweiler! I'll tell you why – the nearest spot to it, and almost equidistant from the freeway, is El Porto, which is always one-to-two-feet higher. The northernmost peak of El Porto is a jetty called Hammerland where it can get *really* big, but also can dump faster than your bowels after that Taco Bell visit on the way back from Malibu. If you continue heading south, you'll cruise through Manhattan Beach, which is about the same, but a tad smaller and more accessible. These two miles of beach attract about 70% of the surfers in Los Angeles (my reckoning, not according to real statistics). The other 30% congregate in Malibu, with some percentage in between heading down to Orange County, up to Ventura, or spreading themselves out amongst the other lesser breaks of Los Angeles – and about .033% of those surfers go to Dockweiler (that math is real).

So why surf there if it's so bad? That's the thing – it's not! Dockweiler breaks very similar to El Porto, but just about a foot or two smaller, which on most of the dumpy, closed out days (so most days), means it can be more manageable than its popular big brother. Include in your consideration smaller crowds, public fire pits and free parking, and you'll see why I love Dockweiler so much. But even based solely on surfing, I've had many, many more fun days at Dockweiler than

El Porto, hands down. And this day, though a bit of a concession overall, was no exception.

We arrived to a larger-than-normal congregation at the first jetty. It breaks to the right here, peeling off the rocks, and despite its tiny reputation, the right swell produces large, clean, fast-breaking waves. This Sunset-turned-Dockweiler morning was an average size, maybe three to four feet, but there were a few right-handers to be had, with the occasional left. I had been noticing through the last couple of years more people discovering Dockweiler as a solid surf spot. It might have been because it is a little more friendly towards beginners than the oft intimidating El Porto, though if you chat with your fellow riders at lifeguard towers 49 and 51, you will meet several rippers who have been riding that wave for years. (If this book sells a million copies, I'm going to go ahead and apologize to those guys right now for the increased influx of surfers who may frequent the beach: I'm sorry.)

We surfed. We had fun. Justin left early (he prefers Porto). Tyler showed up late and swam instead of surfed. Mitchel and Rochelle stayed out and it was a good time. Well, as all good times go, they must come to an end. Most of my surf sessions these days end with that guilty feeling of leaving my wife to watch our two young daughters by herself, and that day was no special case. And so it came time to catch the famed final ride, which would potentially become my last ride at Dockweiler. Ever.

I am nearly tearing up writing that line, such is my love for this location. I lived a mere mile and a half from the spot for a year of my life, which became my favorite home during our tenure in Los Angeles. Big lefts, long rights. Overhead closeouts and tiny surf. Victory and defeat. The beach breaks that comprise that fragile sand hold such a dear place in my heart that the thought of only one final wave there tugs at my heartstrings in a way that threatens to pull it down, right through my rib cage and into my sullen belly. However, if there ever was a last wave for me at Dockweiler, the wave I caught that day was a worthy candidate.

Mitchel and I had decided to catch one more to ride in, while Tyler and Rochelle were out swimming (Ty treaded water for about 45 minutes that day, by the way…the beast), and a nice one rolled in that had Mitchel's name on it. As it swept past, taking Mitchel over the falls in a typical closeout, I had a feeling another one was on its way – a standout, just a little bit farther than where everyone else was sitting. It was as if God himself whispered in my ear to paddle out – *The wave is coming Rick. If you paddle, it will show* – so I did.

And so did the wave.

The second wave in the set swelled up just to the north of the peak of the jetty, where I was in perfect position. It was a long drop, head-high at least, and so I fell into a deep bottom turn. The momentum carried me back up the wave as I swept past Tyler, who was cheering. Rochelle's bobbing head was there too as I turned and headed back down, pumping the wave past surfer after surfer. Mitchel was one of them, paddling back from his closeout. I could feel the energy of these friends, who had been by me in so many sessions at this very break, urging me on as I experienced what became one of the best waves of my life.

Much of the crowd tried to drop in on me on that wave, but somehow they knew it wasn't for them. They pulled out, one by one, as I sped by on my wave of destiny. It wasn't the biggest wave I've ever ridden, or even the best shape. I didn't get barreled and I didn't catch air. But I think God must have sent that one, a little wisp from his lips to say goodbye, tossing the water all those miles down and across the cold Pacific Ocean just for me on this day, where I was so glad my road had unintentionally led to Dockweiler.

Such was my goodbye wave to LA, and so here I sit in my mom's dining room in Charleston, South Carolina, reminiscing already about our seven years of living in Los Angeles, processing through writing, as I often do.

What follows is my account of those seven years, where surfing went from a moderate interest into nothing short of a passion, lifestyle, mirror, teacher, and friend. It contains a balance of anecdotal stories and lessons from the water, as well as practical tips, should you ever want to venture shoreward (which I hope you do), particularly in Los Angeles.

Really, this book is a snapshot of a place and time very dear to me, where experiences on the ocean turned into life lessons which turned into words on a page. Documenting these stories was the most fun thing I have written to-date, and I hope it is just as fun for you to read.

So, let's get started…

PART ONE
EAST MEETS WEST

THE SURF 'N TURK CLUB

GROWING UP ON THE East Coast, we only surfed in the summers when the water temperature made its way above 68 degrees or so. This was a decision mostly influenced by my dad, who taught me how to surf and also hates cold water. And so, when I moved to Los Angeles in July of 2009, an ignorant Southerner wanting to take his mild surfing habits across the country with him as an escape from pursuing filmmaking in the "big city," and the water was cold, I simply waited for it to warm up. August came…still cold. Then September…then October and, unfortunately for me, the water stayed about the same.

It took me longer than it should have to realize what was happening (I hate to admit it, but sometimes I'm a slow learner). It was a different ocean and different convection currents. The Atlantic flows clockwise from the south, carrying the warm Southern water up with it to the grassy beaches of South Carolina, and beyond – even New Jersey surfers wear trunks in the summer. The Pacific, however, flows from the north, bringing the chilled Arctic water down south. As a result, the water temperature really doesn't change all that much – it goes from very cold to kind of cold. And so, when you're watching a show like *The O.C.* or *Baywatch* and they feature guys in March surfing in trunks, it's a bold-faced Hollywood lie. Unless that guy is Ty Pukatch, to whom I owe my first full summer of surfing in California.

Needless to say, having waited so long for the water to warm, I didn't end up surfing too much that first year (I told you I had mild surfing habits back then). In February of the following year, I started interning for Tyler at a production company called Hero Pictures and, after discovering that I "surfed," we decided to go out on the water together for an early morning session.

Tyler preferred Santa Monica out of all the Los Angeles beaches and, despite having a somewhat of a bad reputation amongst surfers; it really isn't all that bad in the morning. If you paddle out before 8:00AM, you can park for free at the meters at Bay Street and Ocean Way (just pay attention to the amazingly convoluted street cleaning signs – a good rule for all of Los Angeles, actually). The waves roll in nice and mellow in the morning as the grey clouds float over-head like giant buoys before the sun heats up the air, dispelling the gloom, bringing in the winds and chopping up the water. I have had several unreasonably fun days at this spot, which is usually reserved for tourists, particularly surfing just south of the famed pier with its roller coaster and Ferris wheel. It made you feel like a real Angeleno watching them turn on the rides as you surfed such a famous beach, the coaster cars gliding empty in preparation for a crowded day full of out-of-towners. There actually is a pleasant little surf crew that frequents this spot and for one summer, we were part of it.

The Wavestorm was always Ty's board of choice. It is a $100, eight-foot piece of Taiwanese foam that somehow rides better than many of the shaped boards I've tried. At the time I was riding the board I grew up on – a Surfboards Hawaii that was designed by a local rider named Norman Godley. It was my dad's board before he gave it to me, and as the story goes, my dad was out in the water one day when a guy did a 360-degree turn around his head. My dad was awestruck. Afterwards, the skilled surfer paddled over and asked my dad how he liked that board. "I love it!" he replied, to which the surfer said, "Good. I designed it!"

And it *was* a nice board – a quick little twin-finned fish that was about as maneuverable as a whitewater kayak. It felt like it had a pivot point right in the middle, and so you could turn in just about any direction at any given moment. The problem with it was I couldn't turn at all!

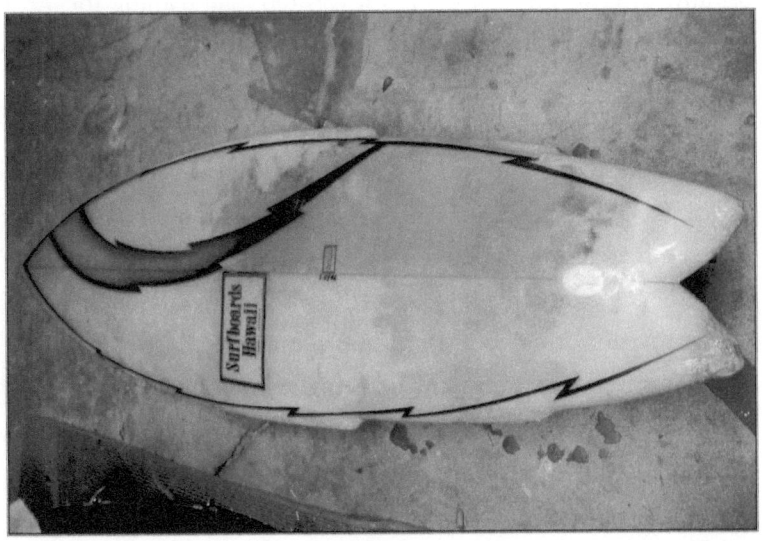

The infamous fish, lightning bolt and everything. (Photo by author)

Learning on a board that squirrelly had its challenges, most of which prohibited me from progressing much as a surfer. It was like hiking your first Colorado fourteener in sandals. I should have started on a big canoe of a surfboard, a nine-foot longboard that would have been harder to flip over than to ride. However, up to that point I had spent most of my time in the water trying to learn on a board I had no business riding for at least two to three years into my surfing career. As a result, I sucked at surfing!

Thankfully, Tyler, in his uniquely youthful wisdom, saw what was happening and offered me a 6'8" Al Merrick that he had picked up second-hand. It was a little too skinny for him, but just about perfect for me (I told you, he's a beast of a man). Before too long I was learning to drop in right and left with confidence, riding the face of the waves instead of the whitewater. Such is a crucial step for any surfer to hit, and though it was too long coming for me, I was glad that it happened.

That summer changed my life really, as it sparked in me the passion for surfing that grew into a full-fledged flame. It didn't take long for our Santa Monica mornings to turn bi-weekly with the occasional weekend session. To this day I am incredibly grateful for that summer and especially for Tyler – if he hadn't gifted me that board, or at least invited me out on the water, who knows if I would even be writing this book right now! (Imagine, Reader, just how sad that would be…) He is an amazing and noteworthy guy; hard worker, dedicated husband, present father, generous friend. But one thing that really stands out about Ty Pukatch, to bring it back to my original topic, is that he never, ever wears a wetsuit!

This man has been known to surf in February with no more covering than a pair of trunks and the hair on his chest. Many times, I paddled out with him in my $35 Maui and Sons spring-suit (from

Costco, everyone's favorite surf shop), shivering in my neoprene and wishing for a sale on full-suits that actually fit me. The only outside source of warmth that Tyler chooses is a couple swigs from a bottle of Wild Turkey Kentucky bourbon and a kiss from his wife. This man is a bear, and it shows.

So, years later, when Tyler started the Surf 'n Turk Club, it was no surprise that "No wetsuits" is listed twice in the group's thirteen written rules. Among them are also, "Take ONE swig and pass (of the aforementioned Wild Turkey)," "Bros before hos," and "If you see the police, you must yell 'PO PO' and, if you are holding the Turk, immediately conceal it." Also listed are "SHARE surfwax" and, "When one man is talking real talk, all others must shut up and show respect."

That is the kind of man Ty Pukatch is, and that is why I am proud to be part of the Surf 'n Turk Club (though my cold-nature and frequent wetsuit use should certainly expel me). It is by the grace of God that we are friends, and a little grace from Tyler's having let such a kook[1] in as a member.

So, if you are thinking of paddling out in Los Angeles, but may be afraid of all those stories about localization and surf gangs, remember: There is at least one good surf crew out there. Its members stand for all that is right and true, protecting the fragile waters of the City of Angels, honoring their brothers and welcoming strangers…just as long as they have whiskey and/or surf wax in tow.

As the saying goes, we're all kooks at one point or another in our lives, and so a certain dose of grace should be handed out, though

---

1 "Kook" is a common surf term for a newbie, or even an experienced surfer who just doesn't "get it." Frequently over-dressed or laden with unnecessary gear, a kook is the kind of surfer who will get in your way on accident or mistakenly neglect to follow common surf rules or courtesy.

even this philosophy has its limits. Keep your head up the next time you're at the beach and when you spot a kook, you'll kind of just… know. And if you don't, well, maybe it's you.

THE WAVESTORM

THE WAVESTORM MADE ITS way into the last piece, and just in case you're a "real surfer" who would never ride such a piece of overseas garbage and are currently considering using this book to start your next beach bonfire, I feel like I need to explain...

I bought one of these cheap foamies from Costco for my wife a few years back and, on a smallish day, I took it out instead of my short board. I have to say I was blown away by how good this eight-foot piece of Taiwanese engineering actually rides. It does take a certain lack of self-consciousness to ride the thing, but I can't deny its prowess, though I am pretty sure that was an accident on the manufacturer's part. I promise I'm not paid by Wavestorm or Costco or some Foam Board Riders Association of the World, but I recommend this board so often that I must be honest with you about why I have such a soft spot for this soft-top:

No shame at Dockweiler. (Photo by Katie Bickerstaff)

I Catch More Waves: It is big and light, so once you've figured out your weight distribution, you'll be able to catch almost anything and I mean *anything.* If you look behind me in that picture above you'll notice that the water is literally flat. I actually caught waves that day with this board – they were miniscule, but I rode them with a smile on my face and imported foam under my feet. The trick is to park just a bit farther out, past everyone else at the break (save the Stand-up Paddleboard riders). You will catch the wave before them and, if they're following proper surf etiquette, they'll back off and you will have the wave to yourself. Then you can shred! (No lie, keep reading...)

It is Surprisingly Maneuverable: I took this to Sunset and PCH on a day when the waves were small but beautiful long right-handers that rode for ages. It's got three fins, so it rides like any thruster and ends up being a surprisingly responsive board (more on what that means and different board types later). I was able to work the face in a very shortboard-esque manner, marking this as the day I fell in love with the Wavestorm. Also, some smart company started making different fins you can switch out from the cheap plastic ones that come with the Wavestorm. So even if you get a little self-righteous on me and say it could *never* properly work a wave, like Settlers of Catan, there are options for expansion (though you don't really need them).

My Leash Never Breaks: The board is thick, and sometimes feels like you're riding some kind of kayak-shovel hybrid. As a result, it's pretty difficult to keep underwater in a good duck-dive. So, when the surf report was inaccurate one day, and four-foot waves were actually eight-foot monsters at Hammerland, I showed up with the Wavestorm and found myself in some dicey situations. I had to ditch the board a few times when some particularly massive closeouts came crashing on me (Poor surf etiquette, I know. I guess that's strike two against this writer…), and though the force of those waves felt like an aquatic herd of horses, my leash never broke. I am honestly dumbfounded by this one, as the leash is little more than rubber, rope, and some Velcro at the end, but I've had several name-brand leashes break under less pressure.

You Can Return Anything to Costco: One of the few downfalls to the Wavestorm is the aforementioned kayak-shovel effect, causing the board to scoop up water sometimes on the drop-in. Well, I noticed that over time these nose-dives were causing the board to bend (particularly when I would lend it to inexperienced riders, which is who the board was pretty much designed for). Well, one day it broke in half, even though it has three stringers (vertical wooden supports inside the board) running through it. My wife had had the board for about two years at that point, so I thought I'd cut my losses and trash it, keeping the leash, stomp pad and a couple fins for future use. Tyler then suggested that I try and return it to Costco, given their extremely loose return policy. With nothing to lose I gave it a shot.

I literally showed up with a two-year-old broken board that looked like I had just pulled it out of a trash can, no receipt, and minus the Costco card I had purchased it with (it was Tyler's)...and walked out with $100. I mean, how are they still in business?! My friend Josh Andrew was with me and so embarrassed when I vaguely explained my situation to the customer service guy that he walked away in shame of association. The funny thing is, he went out and bought the short-board version at Costco not too long after. (Note: I DO NOT recommend the short board – it is a glorified boogey board.)

So that is why I love the Wavestorm, and why I am recommending it to you; particularly if you're a beginner, or someone who frequents a weak break and is looking to have some unashamed fun. The Bible says that God uses the foolish things of the world to shame the wise, so maybe there is a little bit of the divine even in this cheap, crappy surfboard. It is great for Los Angeles riding, and you'll find it at every surf school in town. Of course, on the other side of the spectrum, there are videos of guys riding fifteen-foot waves with this thing, which begs the question: Is this accidentally the best board ever designed, or just another piece of mass-produced junk? Check it out and decide. What do you have to lose except a little pride and $100?!

"But God chose the foolish things of the world to shame the wise; God chose the weak things of the world to shame the strong." (1 Corinthians 1:27, New International Version)

LEARNING TO SURF

LET'S FACE IT: SURFING is a difficult sport. Those that can stand up and ride a wave their first day are few and far between. And rightfully so – you're practically walking on water! Being a skater or snowboarder certainly helps but imagine riding a skate ramp that is constantly changing underneath you; a mini avalanche of sorts...that is surfing.

But people do it and do it well. I am only sometimes one of them, but as my love for surfing grew, a little skill did too. So, I have broken down what I think are the three most helpful wave-catching tips, just in case the stories in this book make you want to paddle out for yourself. They are: *Know your break, Know your board, Know your body*. (It looks like "knowing" is still half the battle...)

Know Your Break: Understanding the spots where you surf is the first step to a successful surf session. Is it big and dumpy? Small, but long rides? Breaking left, right, or both? A beach or rock/reef break? All of these will inform your decision of where, when, and how you should paddle out. Of course, this knowledge comes from a variety of sources: surf reports, locals, videos, personal experience...anything to help increase your awareness of a spot is beneficial.

No matter what, I always watch a set or two come through before paddling out. Too many times I have been over-excited about the session ahead of me, paddled right into a big dumpy set and was subsequently destroyed by wave after wave. By the time the set passed and I made it to the break, I was worn out and my amp-level was very low. Watching other surfers and where the waves break is a crucial part of this first step, and will save you a ton of time and energy. One book I read – Kook, by Peter Heller – advised to watch waves for *at least* thirty minutes before even hitting the water. This feels a little extreme for the guy who barely has an hour to surf most sessions, so I'll just advise a set or two.

Also, always talk to people – to find out information about your spot, *and* to make more surf buddies! It was a game changer when I was surfing at a familiar spot and met a new friend, Russell, who informed me of a channel right next to a jetty that was pretty much a paddle-out-conveyor-belt, getting me to the break in no time! Though I had surfed there many times, I never noticed the channel, which ended up paying off huge when a head-high set came through during my paddle out, poised to obliterate. The extra speed helped me escape certain doom, and my friendship with Russell was thus sealed.

Know Your Board: You saw the picture of my first board and read how I rode it pretty poorly for about *ten years* before Ty gave me something more suited for my skill level. Imagine the time I would have saved had I *not* started on a board that was too short and as squirrely as a Chihuahua on roller skates! Choosing the correct board for the correct day is a huge part of surfing. You also read about the Wavestorm in the last piece too, and I firmly believe that it is a good board to start with that also has the capacity to guide you into riding bigger waves as your skill increases.

Knowing which board is best for the day can make or break your surf session. Again, I advise you to talk to other surfers and observe what they are riding. Good friends will rarely lead you astray. (Finish the chapter for more information on board types. "Bickerstaffs are finishers," I always tell my kids, and for good reason...finishers are rewarded with knowledge!)

Know Your Body: Once you have a board and feel comfortable on it, the next step is developing a physical awareness on the water. The biggest aspect to this is weight distribution. Being able to shift your weight along the board can make a world of difference when it comes to catching more waves and having longer rides. Are you paddling for a wave that just isn't picking you up? Maybe you need to lean forward. Are you nose diving in steep surf? Take a little hop back on the board as you drop in. Keep losing your balance when you stand up? You probably need to bend your knees and stay low.

All of these things are part of feeling your way along the wave and being able to adjust yourself physically to continue riding. Little shifts in your steps and foot adjustments can be the difference between riding a wave to its end or wiping out. And remember, tips will help, but most physical awareness comes from feeling comfortable on your own board and trying out different methods on the wave. So, get out there and start riding!

There are plenty of resources online for more specific surf tips, but as I said earlier, making friends on the waves is the best thing you can do to improve your surfing. And your life!

A bit more on choosing your board: Have you ever been in a conversation with an experienced surfer and heard, "What kind of board do you have?" You pause and break eye contact as insecurities set in…you have no idea what kind of board you have! All you know is that your old roommate left it on the balcony when he moved out. Or maybe you're humble enough to admit, "I don't know," only to hear in reply, "Well, what size is it? What's the tail look like? Where did you get it?"

"Big…round…dumpster…" you reply, as you just realized you described a trashcan, which is where this conversation is heading. Well, my friends, now is the time to learn about your board! Who knows, maybe you've been riding the wrong board all along, and it's time to put that duct taped short board on Craigslist for something more your speed. Or maybe you are a pretty good surfer, but you have never really considered different boards to meet different needs. Either way, here is some information on board shapes, which can *generally* be broken up into five categories: longboard, funboard/egg, shortboard, gun, fish.

Longboards are where most surfers start. They are wide, long (eight-to-twelve-feet) and stable; *and* a good place to gain your confidence on the water. They usually have a single fin, rounded tails and thrive in small surf. Of course, you will sometimes see those old rippers tearing up a wave on a longboard and wonder, *How do they do that on such a big board?* Knowledge is no replacement for time and experience.

Funboard/ Eggs are a great mid-range board when you desire more maneuverability, but still want that stability and ease in catching waves. They are a little shorter than a longboard (six-to-nine-feet) and may have three fins (a thruster), which will help you lock into those bottom turns and such. Eggs are a little shorter, fat, and have a "retro" look. They have become very popular over the last several years, particularly at Los Angeles beaches where the waves aren't that big, though you can still take one of these out and have a lot fun even in small surf.

Shortboards come in handy when you want performance and are ready to sacrifice stability to get it. They are small (less than seven-feet) and thin (my dad calls them "potato chips"), which means you usually need a wave with a little size or swell behind it to really get going. They also typically have three fins (again, a thruster), which helps with maneuverability and stability at the same time.

Guns are long (seven-to-twelve-feet), thin, and typically for really big waves. The average LA surfer doesn't spend too much time on these, in my experience, so neither will I waste precious paper writing about them! Just know and respect what they, and the people who ride them, are designed for and can accomplish.

Fish boards are small (less than seven-feet), wide and typically have a swallowtail (see picture of my first board). Their width helps in small waves, but their design promotes maneuverability. They also often have two or four fins, which I find makes the board a bit more squirrely but will help you turn faster and hit the lip harder!

There are other types of boards of course, but these examples will help you know a bit more about what you are riding, or what might be a good purchase for where and how you surf. It is also a good idea to have a couple different boards in your quiver (what surfers call their stash of boards), because you never know when a massive swell is going to hit your hometown, even when it is typically tiny. If that's the case, grab a rack to store your beauties, because they can stack up!

P.S. - I got started in writing about surfing through a yearlong stint as a blogger for StoreYourBoard.com; hence that last line about the rack. This book wouldn't be complete without a shout-out to my first literary employer! Also, most of the information in this piece is thanks to research from Tactics (www.tactics.com) and Surf Science (www.surfscience.com). I hope it is helpful!

FIREPITS

I AM A BIG fan of *The O.C.* Yes, that may diminish my continually wavering notability as a trustworthy source on surfing and Southern California, but at least I am honest and that has to count for something. If it helps, I didn't love it when it was on the air (although I was always a fan of the music they used). This show grew on me during my first year in Los Angeles when, before the age of readily available online streaming, my roommates started going through the series on DVD. Well, the next thing you know I am wrapped up in the teenage melodrama of fictional Orange County, and the whole stupid thing has wedged itself into my soft little heart.

If you are a fan like me, or maybe just watched a few episodes, you have likely seen some beach bonfires where all the cool kids get together and hang out, partake in some illegal drinking, and maybe even find love…or the soft illusion of loved masked in a dramatic teenage romance. There is usually some long-haired hippie playing guitar and singing a Dave Matthews song (as long as the producers paid to cover it), and usually a fight or two once the new kid shows up to cause a ruckus. Well, maybe you watched these scenes and wondered if they are truly possible in Southern California, and the answer is yes! Sort of...

Probably the best thing about Dockweiler Beach is the long rows of firepits that line the beach. It is part of the California State Parks system, and as far as I know is the only place you can legally have a fire on the beach in LA county. I have spent dozens of afternoons and evenings at Dockweiler bonfires, hanging with friends, partaking in *legal* drinking, eating hot dogs and s'mores and, of course, surfing. I did not find love (I already had it) but did watch a romantic sunset or two with my wife...and the occasional surf buddy. No fights broke out because, hey – we're peace-loving surfers and we don't do that!

"Blessed are the peacemakers, for they shall be called sons of God." *(Matthew 5:9 NASB)*

The funny thing about this magical place is that many people in Los Angeles don't even know it exists! The first time I heard about Dockweiler was in a job interview for an artsy summer camp. The boss told me that at the end of the season they all have a big bonfire at Dockweiler, partying it up while thundering planes take off overhead from LAX. That sounded amazing to me at the time, and so I logged it as a potential weekend get-together if I ever got the gumption to organize one. Well, one appeared to me shortly thereafter when Tyler had a birthday party at the beach. As I said, I usually followed Ty wherever he asked me to go, and so when I showed up at the end of the 105 freeway without knowing where I was, it didn't take long to realize that I had been made privy to one of the great jewels of Southern California, the same one alluded to me in that failed job interview just a few short months before.

We built a "manopy" on Ty's birthday, creating a makeshift tent out of PVC pipes and a tarp (it worked...sort of). Then we ate food, before eating more food, and then later we had some food – much of it was cooked over the fire, which was on and off as the day progressed. A couple of our friends had bought a sailboat and got it as close to shore as possible. Of course, Tyler decided to swim out to it, but the Coast Guard showed up and told them they couldn't swim that far, which only strengthened Ty's resolve. I don't remember if he made it or not, but the blatant disregard for authority showed me that this man, though not a skateboarder, had some rebel in his heart.

That was the first of many Dockweiler beach days, most of which were filled with multiple surf sessions. If you are thinking of organizing your own firepit beach day, the best thing to do is get to the beach super early, especially in the summer – those firepits fill up fast – though getting there early is of little consequence because the waves are best before the sun rises high and burns off the marine layer ("June Gloom" as they call it).

One time I volunteered to reserve the firepit for a church beach day and was surprised to find a rather large, intriguing looking black plastic bag floating in place. A little more investigation revealed a beached seal that, for some reason, could not get back in the water. I watched as animal control pulled up, took a few cell phone pictures, and then netted the bested beast, dragging it back to a covered truck bed before taking off to an undisclosed, ultra-secret location – maybe where they train seals to be secret spies for the government or something. I was the only one there to see it, but it certainly made for a good story when the sleepers-in found their way to the beach I had so proudly reserved.

Speaking of sea animals, Dockweiler is actually an amazing spot for wildlife. Nearly every visit I see some combination of dolphin, seal, fish, and maybe even something bigger...(That's subtle foreshadowing, folks, so don't stop reading!) The first time we encountered dolphins in the water was one such bonfire beach day when I was out in the water with Aaron and Berk. Both men are excellent at every sport they try, which is somewhat surprising considering how massively tall Berk is (tall people, like myself, aren't always good at surfing due to our high center of gravity). A pod of dolphins was swimming alarmingly close and instead of staying put and letting them do their thing (safety!), Berk decided to paddle towards the fish and see if he could catch a ride. Of course, his lanky arms still were no match for Echo's fin, but I was surprised at his boldness. That same day a similar fin was fast approaching me from the side and I froze. It dipped under water and I half expected it to launch over me, *Free Willy* style. The fin disappeared and I slowly loosened up. A healthy respect for marine life is in the heart of every surfer, though I'll admit mine is coupled with fear.

Yes, this beach truly is the embodiment of what a good California summer should look like, and my humble stories are just a sampling of what you can experience. If you park in the free spaces up on Vista Del Mar though, make sure you leave by 10pm or YOU WILL GET TICKETED! The police there are simply ruthless; but I like to think they are merely guarding this jewel of the Pacific out of the goodness in their hearts. Although $75 per ticket is a little steep, even for Dockweiler...

THE STARSHIP SURFERS OF ANARCHY

I WROTE ABOUT THE Surf 'n Turk club earlier, but there is an officially unofficial surf club that precedes it – *The Starship Surfers of Anarchy*. This elusive group was formed on the dirty sands of Venice Beach, after not a few early-morning surf sessions. Comprised of myself, Korey, Danny, and occasionally his brother Mikey, the SSoA roamed the beach in search of...well, really, we just roamed the beach. A very small patch of beach at that, now that I think of it.

We chose Venice because Korey and Danny liked it. I am still not sure why – the break is okay but the parking is terrible. Maybe it was the history. Maybe it was the nearby skatepark right on the beach. Or maybe it was the abundance of sun tanning women that brought this epic group to the West Coast stage, where all things weird come to perform. Either way, it was a fun summer riding with these guys and forming the brotherhood known as the Starship Surfers.

Venice does indeed have a storied history in the surfing world. For me, as a California-dreamin' kid from South Carolina, it was first made known in the film *Lords of Dogtown* and its preceding documentary *Dogtown and Z Boys*. The beginning of western surf and skate culture owes a large portion of its foundation to Venice, and it still lives up to the name. It is the favored spot of my hippiest friend Josh Andrew who, though not a Starship Surfer, is more a Venice-beacher than anyone I know. One trip here and you will know what I mean…

As far as surfing goes, the break is a right-hander that peels off the south side of the breakwater jetty. Sometimes you can catch waves on the north side, but they break so close to the beach that you just might break your neck too. Back on the south side, the paddle out is so long that it is really like two waves: beginner and intermediate. As a result, this is a great place to learn to surf. You can rent a board from any number of "surf shops" (glorified beach rentals) on the strand, and then try your luck at paddling out.

Actually, my first time surfing in California was at Venice, with rented boards from one such stand. They were crappy, glass-heavy boards from the 80s that the shop owner probably found in someone's dumpster in the neighborhood spanning several blocks from the beach (a good place to park, by the way). It was October and we didn't know the West Coast was cold, being the naïve East Coast surfers we were. It was cold. Very cold.

The other good thing about the short break is that it rarely gets above three feet deep, so you can stand up and learn to surf that way. This was excellent for Danny who, though a solid surfer, preferred to never paddle out past where he could stand up due to a childhood trauma involving a rip current. Poor guy.

My sister, contemplating the cold water in 2003.
(Photo by Rick Bickerstaff, Jr.)

If you are brave enough to paddle to the bigger break, you can catch some nice dumpy right-handers, with the occasional left as the break is wide and sometimes creates an A-frame of sorts (A-frame = a wave that breaks in both directions. That is a very *generous* description of Venice, by the way; A-frames are usually reserved for pristine waves in exotic locations). I have seen folks shred here, including my friend Nelson, who tore up some mellow lefts on an egg shape during a cold and cloudy session that I will never forget. I have yet to surf with him since, mostly because I'm still intimidated by how good he was…

Overall, you can have a good time at Venice, so you need to check it out at some point in your surfing career. If the waves are bad, there is always the amazing skatepark right on the beach, which has two killer bowls, a snake run, and a fun street course. Legend is in the air at this location, and I am proud to say that the Starship Surfers of Anarchy claim just a tiny piece of that atmosphere, whether we deserve it or not.

It was after one such session with the Starship Surfers that I wrote this song, one of my first about surfing. Check out the accompanying album to this humble book, downloaded or streaming, and enjoy "Golden Coast Summertime." It's one to add to your "Beach Playlist," capturing a bit of the magic to be found on the Southern California shoreline.

GOLDEN COAST SUMMERTIME

You know the sun will soon
Burn off that June gloom
And the West Coast swell
Will be here soon
As we cruise to the beach
In the afternoon
Hop on in, take a ride
Golden coast summer time

There's a girl at home
And she's waiting
For the sun to come out
Now she's thinking
That the Left Coast's
Calling her name and
All she needs, is a ride
Golden coast summer time

And the sun shines
On the Pacific
Blue like her eyes
Next to soft lips
And you're holding her
Close when the breeze hits
When she smiles, watch her shine
Golden coast summertime

Woah, you know we're
All out here for a reason
Woah, and I think
It's time to start living
Woah, we were meant
To be together
Woah, shine like
Golden coast weather

You've been sitting scared
For a long time
Watching the waves
Hit the shoreline
Don't only get wet
During high tide
Grab a board, take a ride
Golden coast summertime

And the sun sinks past the horizon
As we warm ourselves
By the bonfire
Life's good when
We are together
Live in love, feeling fine
Golden coast summertime

SALTWATER HEALS

IT'S TRUE. HAVE YOU ever had a cut or sore that just wouldn't go away, and then paddled out for a nice long surf session, only to have it disappear a couple short days later? The first time I experienced this on a significant level was the summer after my freshman year of high school. I was cutting bushes at my grandfather's house and somehow walked away with this gnarly, oozy rash about three inches long and a quarter-inch thick. Here's a picture for reference:

Just kidding – I wouldn't do that to you.

We're still not sure if I just had some allergic reaction to a plant, or if a poisonous caterpillar got me, but the thing didn't leave...all summer. Thankfully I wasn't doing too well with the ladies back then, so it didn't hinder me in that department, and it also got me off the hook for cutting bushes for pretty much the rest of my life. However, no matter what we tried, the thing just wouldn't heal. That is, until, I went surfing.

I regret to say that I wasn't much of a surfer in those days. I grew up doing it fairly often with my dad, but after a big thick glass-heavy surfboard from the 80s hit me in the head when I was eight or nine years old, I had just about sworn it off. I got really into skateboarding at age thirteen, and so that became my main passion for all of high school and into college (and after college and into my thirties, if we're being honest). Still close to surfing, but still a little different. So yes, I went a whole summer without surfing and then, at the end, had a session that mystically healed my arm. I went to school with confidence that year, and later got a girlfriend. Coincidence? I think not.

Since that experience, I always try my best to surf when some topical illness plagues me. Sorry, that sounds like I have leprosy – no, just cuts and bug bites mostly. I mean, I'm *always* trying to surf anyway, but I make a little more effort to go out in infirmary. But while in California I noticed something interesting: the saltwater heals just a little less out West.

I didn't do any research into the salinity of the Atlantic vs. the Pacific, and I am hoping some knowledgeable reader will write me a letter to explain to me why the Pacific doesn't have the healing power that the Atlantic does (you call it laziness, I call it audience interaction). It could be all the gross, polluted water in LA County – I have often snagged a piece of trash and tucked it in my wetsuit to do my part to de-litter the Los Angeles water. More often, I've walked away with a big piece of tar on my foot or board. It is common knowledge in Los Angeles that you should *never* surf after a rain, because practically half of the city has washed its weeks and months of built-up street-gunk into the ocean. I think this a terrible design for storm drains, but way-back-when I guess they didn't care that much about destroying the earth. (Good thing it's different now, right? *RIGHT?!*)

Either way, this is my experience and like a good pseudo-Millennial, I will mark said experience as truth. And so, like the

Pool of Bethesda, I will try my best to dip into these life-giving hallows whenever the Angel of Swell should decide to churn up the waters into some rideable waves. I hope you find the same true for you too! But even if you don't get your rash removed by a dip or two in the sea, you will nonetheless be happier because you surfed. So, it is either a win-win or maybe just a win. I will take those odds to Vegas any day.

See how good of a thing surfing is?

"The earth is the Lord's, and everything in it,
the world, and all who live in it;
for He founded it on the seas
and established it on the waters."
(Psalm 24:1-2)

PART TWO
LOVE

WHEN I FALL IN LOVE

I FELL IN LOVE with my wife Katie pretty quickly. We had met at a music festival in October of 2008, and by Valentine's Day the following February, we said the "L word." (You know, the first "L word" before that other "L word" was a TV show.) She was just so easy to fall in love with: definitely one of the most fun people I've ever known with a generous heart and beauty to match.

I heard a pastor once say he tried to use the word "love" sparingly around his daughters, to keep it a special description, reserved only for those things that really matter (as in avoiding phrases like, "I love mac and cheese"). I think that is a good idea, but I also readily say that I love Taco Bell, the band Five Iron Frenzy, and the movie *3 Ninjas*. But I think I really *do* love those things, and they also grabbed my heart quickly.

Still, I don't fall in love with *everything* that easily, oh no. My love affair with surfing took quite a bit longer for some reason (about fifteen years), but I remember the season I realized it was real, and the "L word" sprung from my heart like a fountain of saltwater.

"And now these three remain: faith, hope, and love.
But the greatest of these is love." (1 Corinthians 13:13)

It was late summer in 2010. I had made good money working at Huntington Beach High School teaching video/audio classes for a few summer sessions, and so I set aside some for an engagement ring for Katie. I then quit my job to pursue something closer to town (HB was about 45 miles away). Since I had a season of abundance, I decided to take my time finding a job, intending to focus on my writing/filmmaking career. But do you know what I did instead of working hard? Surfed and skated. Just about every day.

The funny thing about it all is that I moved to Los Angeles to pursue film, and here I was given a golden opportunity to really invest in that pursuit. Not having to worry about a job (for a short time anyway), I could have written and shot and edited plenty of projects. To be fair, I did finish one movie, *:The Everything After.* (But it really wasn't that good – you can look it up on YouTube. And no, that's not a typo in the title.)

The days were just too warm and the breeze was too cool. The waves were inviting and I was exploring, so I kept paddling out. I couldn't help it. And that's when I realized what my true love really was.

This epiphany was confirmed years later when I was given a rare opportunity through my alumnus, the Los Angeles Film Studies Center, to attend a "Writing for Television" seminar – for free! The problem was that it occurred the same day as the Switchfoot BroAm, a surf contest and outdoor concert that I had just found out about and really wanted to attend. I love the band Switchfoot (there's that word again) and love outdoor concerts even more. I once got the opportunity to see Switchfoot play at the US Open of surfing in

Huntington Beach right on the water, and so I was itching at the opportunity to do it again. There was also a band I enjoy called Run River North opening, and so the reasons were stacking for me to ditch the career convention and go surfing instead.

I struggled with the decision all week, but something inside told me I should really go to the TV seminar. Maybe I would meet someone who believed in my writing, find a collaborator, or pick up some tips to get my still floundering career going. But the plans for heading south to the BroAm were solidifying with Mitchel and Rochelle, and the idea to stop at Trestles (one of my favorite SoCal surf spots) on the way heavily swayed me in that direction. Eventually, my flesh overcame my spirit and I decided to surf instead, rescinding my ticket. I just couldn't help it – the idea of spending a day inside a big dark conference room listening to people talk sounded way too boring compared to a sunny surf adventure. I even justified it by bringing my camera, promising myself I would shoot a video and write a piece about the whole thing on my blog, which I was working hard to incorporate into my career at the time.

The surf adventure turned out to be a bust though. The waves were terrible at Trestles, so we tried surfing at Dana Point, new to all of us, where we rode mediocre waves on a crowded sunny beach day. We hit unusually bad traffic after that and missed Run River North. I shot some video, but it was pretty weak and is still sitting in a folder on a hard drive somewhere, far from making it to the blog. We did catch Switchfoot and it was, of course, a good show. I also got to meet one of my favorite surfers, Rob Machado, which was awkward and amazing at the same time. (I am not sure he knew what was happening when I went up to him and told him he was one of my favorite surfers. "Okay," was the response I received. I don't know, maybe he's used to hearing that… If you're reading this

Rob, it's still true.)

Right choice or not, the whole thing was just a solidification of what I had been suspecting for years: my love for surfing had superseded my love for filmmaking. This is dangerous ground when you relocated thousands of miles away in the name of said career, but return with only a board under your arm, sandy feet, and a good tan to show for it. But the truth is the truth. In pursuit of one passion, I found a truer one in surfing. I might not make a million dollars off of it, but hey, you're reading this book and it wouldn't be here without the sport. (Now go tell all of your friends to buy it so I can justify all that time on the water. Please.)

So, if you got this book to see if surfing might be for you, I have a warning: it just may take over your life. Readers beware! But you also might find true love out on the water, even if it replaces something you only *thought* you loved; or maybe just loved less. I guess that's why the Greeks had several words for "love." Maybe surfers need to invent their own expression of how they feel about riding waves...

"Totally brah, that last one was a gnarly broheme."

Maybe not.

In honor of my wife, I thought I would also share the first song I ever wrote for her, an acoustic version that is on the accompanying record.

MORE BEAUTIFUL

Lately, I've been noticing the leaves
And how they look so green
I'm starting to think
That maybe you're to blame
And how the sky, it looks so blue
Could it be that you
Simply make my world
More beautiful?

And I know you make my world
More beautiful
And I see every day you are
More beautiful
And you turn even stormy skies
More beautiful
And I thank God for making you
More beautiful for me

Lately I've been noticing the stars
Have been falling like my heart
I think that they're trying
To get closer to you
So pick up all the pieces
That you find
Take the ones that are mine
Add my heart to yours
And we'll be beautiful

And even though I know alone
You are so beautiful
I think together we could be
More beautiful
And I will go as far to say
That we could change the world
'Cause I know it's rare to find
Someone as beautiful as you

TINY SURF

"WHY IS IT SO fun to chase tiny surf?" I asked Mitchel as we paddled out into two-to-three-foot sets at Dockweiler. It is a paradox for sure, but as I sat waist deep in the cool early-June Pacific waters, gazing out to a flat horizon, hoping for some sort of swellular disruption, I couldn't help but feel something like happiness.

I like to say that every surfer at some point remarks, "It's good just to be out in the water," and on this day it was more than true. The morning was peaceful and overcast, with a slight drizzle of refreshment that would flare from time to time. It was quiet, as we essentially had the break to ourselves (crowd diminishing: one very good thing about small waves), and though I spent the first twenty minutes of my time in the water reminiscing about the multiple head-high days I had had at that very same spot, I was struck by the bliss and contentment that washed over me like the closeout of nearly every wave I caught.

It looks bigger when you get low! (Photo by Katie Bickerstaff)

The joy that morning was a good reminder of why we surf: not to catch the biggest and best waves, but for fun, for introspection, for community. To enjoy nature as a group of wave riders searching for a life of balance, a part of which *must* include small days. For if every session were ten-foot barrels of glass rolling in never-ending sets on sunny California afternoons, would we even recognize them as perfection? Or would the callous of perpetual fortune cover up our capacity to enjoy both the good and the bad? For what is gold if there is no dirt, and what are barrels if there are no closeouts?

Small waves are a gentle reminder to accept what we are given with humble gratitude, knowing that we have no control over the swells of nature. You can chase waves to the ends of the earth or stay put and complain about your lackluster home break; but the man of contentment will enjoy them both. On this day I was that man of contentment, and on this day I was happy.

"But godliness with contentment is great gain. For we brought nothing into the world, and we can take nothing out of it. But if we have food and clothing, we will be content with that." (1 Timothy 6:6-8)

"I am not saying this because I am in need, for I have learned to be content whatever the circumstances. I know what it is to be in need, and I know what it is to have plenty. I have learned the secret of being content in any and every situation, whether well fed or hungry, whether living in plenty or in want. I can do all this through him who gives me strength." (Philippians 4:11-13)

GOOD PEOPLE

GOOD PEOPLE ARE HARD to find. Not in the sense that the whole world is bad or anything, but just that good people, *really* good people, are kind of rare. I mean "salt of the earth" kind of people; the ones you meet and instantly feel a soul-connection with. When you speak you are completely understood, and when they reply, you take every word like a gold nugget of verbal wealth. The problem with these people is that just about everyone else who meets them feels the same way, so when you *do* find one, you better get in line! As a result, these folks are in high demand and there is only so much time for them to share their goodness with the world, including you.

Two of those good people are my friends Nate and Amy. We were in a church small group together that my wife and I hosted during that fateful time I mentioned earlier as my favorite year for surfing in Los Angeles. We lived close to Dockweiler (less-than two miles away), and I was able to catch surf sessions before *and* after work on a regular basis, not to mention it was one of the biggest winters I still have ever experienced. Nate and I planned to surf many times, but it never happened. We did skate together once for about fifteen minutes on the sidewalk in front of our little duplex in Westchester, just north of LAX. He was a street skater from the 90s and taught me what a proper pressure flip looked like. Nate and Amy were also the people who introduced my wife and I to *Point Break*, which they laud as one of their favorite movies of all time; and I believe it, because I have never seen anyone quote a movie so accurately all the way through.

So, what classifies Nate and Amy as "good people?" They are genuine, caring, and responsible, have a great marriage and are natural mentors. I was at a point in life when I was trying hard to climb the tiny ladder set before me in corporate entertainment. Nate was the guy who told me that he and his friends had worked themselves ragged doing the same thing throughout their twenties and got to thirty, realizing it was a waste of time. Standing in line to get ice cream sandwiches at Diddy Riese in Westwood, he told me that if he won the lottery he would give it all away...*all* of it. And I believe him! They are middle-aged by now, and still listen to punk music and go to shows regularly. They are wise with their time and investments, but never let it get in the way of their faith and values. Fun, hardworking, devoted, faithful, generous, and honest; I am still thankful for the limited time we had together in our tiny living room once a week to talk, pray, and share our lives.

As I wrote earlier though, people like this are hard to come by, and when you do find one (much less two!), everyone else is vying for their time as well. We often spoke of going to the beach to catch a surf, but the only time we ever came close was a short session at Topanga Beach in Malibu – their favorite beach at the time. I had never been there to my knowledge (although it is possible I got dragged there at some time or another without knowing it during my season of blindly following Tyler on surf adventures).

Nate unfortunately declined to surf that day – I don't remember why – but I paddled out on the Wavestorm, as the waves were pretty small and I wanted to actually ride something that day. Topanga is a rocky point break (fitting, given the company) with typically two spots where you can catch the wave. It is almost always overcrowded and localized, but creates a long right that is easy to catch and easier to ride. The paddle out isn't as bad as the one at Malibu pier (a few miles up the PCH), and it is also quite a bit closer to Los Angeles, making it the first really good spot to hit if you are traveling north (though Sunset and PCH is a strong contender, in my book).

I remember surfing the second break and catching quite a few waves that day, which kind of pleased me because I knew my good friend was watching. I talk like such a career surfer sometimes that I'm not always sure my skills can back it up – not in a bragging kind of way, but I just love surfing so much and it comes up so often, that people assume I'm good. "Competent" is a better word than good, although I've found that skill levels tend to be relative terms. I caught several waves that day and I remember Nate telling me that he was impressed at my surfing skills. I genuinely objected to his compliment, but deep down was glad to improve my reputation as a surfer, particularly with someone I respected so much. (Many years later, he *still* tells people I am a really good surfer, though that remains the only day he has ever witnessed me on the water.)

The only other thing I remember from that day is that I dropped in on an older guy on purpose, because I thought I could get ahead of him on the wave – like I said, it's a long mellow right, so the face of the wave has lots of room (though somehow never enough for all the surfers that frequent it). The guy was pretty far to my left and I was sure I was fast enough to get ahead of him. I dropped, pumped and he yelled at me, which threw me off and caused me to fall, then causing him to fall. Lose, lose. I still hold to this day that if he hadn't said anything, we would have both ridden that wave to glory, but that's only speculation.

As I paddled back he told me to never drop in on people. I asked him if he thought he could have caught up to me. He said it's just best to be safe in that regards. The whole discourse kind of made me mad (although later in life I learned that I did not, in fact, have as fast a takeoff as I thought, so he was likely right), but the funny thing was that, when I described the conversation to Nate, he completely had my back. It didn't matter if that guy was right or wrong, my friend stood up for me. Just another reason to salute these two good people, and another reason that I think favorably enough on Topanga Beach to include it in this book.

"A friend loves at all times, and a brother is born for a time of adversity." (Proverbs 17:17)

A MOONSET ROMANCE

"HOW IS IT THAT some of the most romantic moments of my life have been with other men?" Mitchel said with a wry smile. He was referencing the pale moon setting over the Pacific horizon while we caught another morning session before work at Dockweiler. Simultaneously, the bright yellow sun was rising over the LAX airport with brilliant, blinding rays while we paddled for the smallish waves. From east to west, surrounded by beauty.

Too bad our wives weren't there.

It is a funny thing to think about, but surfing innately includes so much beauty. I've seen waves rolling with whitewater wisping off the top, sprinkling you like a little shower of love from the sea. I have probably watched just as many sunsets while surfing as I have in everyday life, or at least really enjoyed them (in between waves, of course). I have paddled next to dolphins and seals, been surprised by pelicans diving for fish just a few yards away, felt the warm wind of a summer day and watched storms brew offshore – and all of that usually with other guys. It brings more weight to the term "bromance," doesn't it?

Mitchel's wife Rochelle does surf though, so sometimes he gets to live out the beauty with the one he loves. And she is a powerhouse on the water, by the way. I've seen her paddle out in huge waves on a board totally unsuited for the ride and somehow hang in the lineup. A truly valiant woman she is.

My wife Katie surfs sometimes as well. One summer in 2013, I witnessed her best wave to-date as she caught a long rolling right in the Outer Banks of North Carolina. She was pregnant with our first daughter though, and so I talked her out of surfing anymore for the sake of our unborn child. Another child less than two years later kept her out of the water, though we did have a nice trip to Pavones in Costa Rica where we enjoyed a session together when the kids were young. Her time is coming though, don't you worry! She'll learn to shred, as she has always wanted to, and then I can rip this page out of the book in a ten-year revised edition, just as she rips up waves left and right.

But until then, my sunsets are seasoned with sausage, if you know what I mean. That's fine with me though, because nature will be beautiful with or without you there to notice it. Surfing will still be fun and good friends will always make it better. Wives can make it *even* better, and kids bring another plane of enjoyment, though for now mine stick to boogie boarding.

The last two pieces were about brotherhood and community, so I thought it might be nice to include a little more inspiration on the topic, because this is something that few people find, but everyone really needs, especially in Los Angeles.

This city is big and there are people everywhere, but it is also one of the loneliest places I have ever encountered. I have met countless transplants who moved to LA without knowing a soul and suffered the consequences of a very solitary life, even while surrounded by millions. Moving to LA for me was a bit different, however, as I had something of a built-in community through my filmmaking program, The Los Angeles Film Studies Center, which you read about in the Foreword by my once-roommate Peter Harmon. When I made the jump to the City of Angels, I did so with four roommates lined up, all fellow alumni (even though I only knew one of them). As a result, we immediately had a gang of friends built in to our living situation.

But what if you didn't know anyone in town and moved here solo? Making friends at work is a pretty good option, or maybe joining a softball or kickball league, both of which I and my wife have done respectively. Of course there is surfing and the dudes and dudettes that come along with it, which by now you know how I feel about. Out of all of it, though, I would say finding a good church can be the most crucial step to finding friends in this city that can be dark and difficult.

I was also lucky in that, amongst my roommates and their friends, most of us attended the same church, Ecclesia Hollywood, which met in the old Pacific Theater right on Hollywood Boulevard – a beautiful and ornate old theater where movie studios used to have their premieres way back in the Golden Age of film. The church had developed into a strong community that was always growing, and I think the main reason for this is that it was a very genuine group of people with little pretense about them.

As you can imagine, even a church in Los Angeles can be filled with an extra dose of ego, and I have certainly been to such places.

But Ecclesia, despite the old-Hollywood lavish in its location, felt very different. Regular people who genuinely cared about their walk with God, along with others' well-being, went to this church. Sure, there were successful actors, writers, and other industry professionals in the congregation, but even the most famous would have a conversation with you. Sounds magical, right? It was.

There are these verses in the book of Acts that are famous in church because they pretty much describe a utopian community, united and devoted and giving in everything for the good of each other. It is something of a target or dream for most church plants. I can't say Ecclesia was exactly one such place, but it came about as close to it as I have ever experienced.

"They devoted themselves to the apostles' teaching and to fellowship, to the breaking of bread and to prayer. Everyone was filled with awe at the many wonders and signs performed by the apostles. All the believers were together and had everything in common. They sold property and possessions to give to anyone who had need. Every day they continued to meet together in the temple courts. They broke bread in their homes and ate together with glad and sincere hearts, praising God and enjoying the favor of all the people. And the LORD added to their number daily those who were being saved." (Acts 2:42-47)

Sounds nice, doesn't it? How powerful would a place like that be in your own life? How about its effect on a community, neighborhood, city, and maybe even state?

One of the last things Jesus prayed over his disciples was for their unity, and not just them, but the rest of his followers for all time also:

"My prayer is not for them alone. I pray also for those who will believe in me through their message, that all of them may be one, Father, just as you are in me and I am in you. May they also be in us so that the world may believe that you have sent me." (John 17:20-21)

Did you catch the significance there? The unity of Jesus' followers is the method through which the world will know that he is who he claimed he was. Can you imagine a more important reason for community?!

Furthermore, the presence of God is guaranteed in it.

"For where two or three gather in my name, there am I with them." *(Matthew 18:20)*

What a promise! We can meet with the God of the universe just by gathering in Christ's name! And so I hope you find a place to worship God and encounter community in genuine ways with genuine people. It won't always be easy or clean (people are *always* messy), but it will always be worth it, in this life and the next.

If you do happen to be searching for a place of worship in Los Angeles, my good friend (and fellow surfer) Matt has created a website where he checks out and shares information on local churches. He is a former pastor, very educated, and maintains a wide skill set both in and outside of the church. Check out what he's created at www.FindingGodinLA.com.

BEACH BREAK BLUES

I HAVE SPENT MOST of my life surfing beach breaks, the first years being at Folly Beach's Tenth Street or the famous Washout, a spot created when a hurricane wiped out a row of houses on the beachfront of Folly Island (*"The wise man builds his house upon the rock..."*). The first surf trip I ever took was with my family to the Outer Banks of North Carolina, where we hit a couple beach breaks in the summer – not their big season, unfortunately, and so no glassy barrels were there to greet us. California is filled with rocky reef breaks, but is no stranger to beach breaks itself, and to be honest, I eventually hit a point where I was getting tired of the downfalls:

- Closeouts
- Backwash waves
- Dredging
- Parking/ Crowds

Most days, I didn't have time to drive up to the nearest point or reef break, and so a quick session at the nearest beach would have to suffice. But if you, radical readers, find yourself in this same situation, fear not, as your humble author has compiled a list of ways to make the most out of your less-than-perfect beach break.

Closeouts are my biggest enemy in surfing. I mean, how are you supposed to get any better at maneuvers when the wave is finished half-a-second after you stand up? The bright side is, if you are used to managing corners on closeouts (corner = the subtlest part of the wave, just ahead of the break), should you ever approach a finely crafted face, you will be in excellent standing to shred.

Some tips I have found are to cut upwards a little immediately after you stand, not fully dropping in to the bottom of the wave, which gets you ahead of the break. Sometimes it is also appropriate to stand up a bit earlier than you think you should. As always, pay plenty of attention to the spot where you catch the wave – ten yards can be the difference between a long ride or a dump right in your face. Of course, sometimes you're either in the right spot or you're not, so you must take what you can get and not get upset, as I tell my children (and myself, from time to time)

It was nice while it lasted... (Photo by Brian Esquivel)

Backwash is when the angle of the beach is so steep that the water gains momentum on its way *back* to the ocean, creating a little mini-wave heading out to sea that can become quite the speed bump. Many times I have been paddling into a wave when one of these hit, slapping me in the face and disorienting me so much that I tumbled down like a dog on an ice rink. I have also been riding standing up while encountering one of these, which is fun when it launches you in the air, but again, ruins your wave.

There isn't much you can do about these except anticipate a disruption in your wave riding experience. Expectations are the father of disappointment, so if you're on the lookout for this backwards phenomenon, it's harder to get mad when it happens.

Dredging can absolutely ruin a spot. This is when they suck sand from under the water just off the beach, and move it up to the beach surface, "renourishing" it. There is a whole host of bad things dredging can do, one of which is completely change your surf spot! The only good thing about dredging that I can figure is that it sometimes forces you to find a new break that you otherwise may not have explored. I suppose it also keeps your beach from completely eroding away…but if the beach got smaller, it would mean fewer crowds, right? Which brings me to my next point:

Parking and crowds are not unique to beach breaks, but definitely more common in my experience. Sometimes the beaches that make good waves aren't accessible or attractive to the typical beach goer, which is awesome for surfers. However, as I mentioned earlier, circumstances may force you to a nearby, familiar and/or popular spot, resulting in a $10 parking fee and 30-minute line waiting for an open space.

Dockweiler on a busy sunny day. (Photo by Katie Bickerstaff)

My advice here? Get a convertible, some good music and embrace patience. Another tip is to talk to other surfers – I have had fellow riders who like to fight the system (!) give me their paid-parking slip as they left the beach. It is also a personal passion of mine to find and share free parking, which is another reason I always preferred Dockweiler Beach and its ample street parking.

A good rule of thumb with beach breaks is that they are always best before 10:00AM, at least in Southern California (but maybe the whole world?). That time is when the wind seems to always pick up and chop up the glassy mounds you've been riding since dawn. But no matter when you can get out or where, I will reiterate: it is always good to get out on the water. Beach break or not, make the most of your circumstances and have fun surfing!

Did that chapter just inspire you to find a crappy beach break and surf? Does this book also inspire you to fly out to Los Angeles and borrow a Wavestorm? Did you spend all your money renting a convertible Mustang and are now forced to find free parking? If so, here is a list of beach breaks in LA worth visiting, and where to park when you get there!

Dockweiler: You can pay $10 to park in the County Parks lot (it's even less on a weekday), which is good if you are having a barbecue and have tons of gear to drag. There was a time – the time when the stories in this book took place – when you could park up top on the street. It was free from 6:00AM to 10:00PM, though the local law enforcement was quite strict about that end-time, resulting in more than a few tickets because of it. On weekends, the cops lined up with tow trucks at 9:30PM, just to ruin everyone's beach bonfires I'm sure...

The other caveat involved in street parking at Dockweiler was that you had to walk down a steep incline to get to the beach. I have done it holding two boards and a wetsuit, as well as with my infant daughters (one at a time of course), so it's not that bad for the nimble and slightly adventurous. As of the date of publishing this book, however, most of this free parking has been removed, save about eight spots across the street and in front of a playground. If you're lucky enough to find one of these, you can make the harrowing journey across a busy four-lane street and *then* climb down the hill. I don't recommend this with kids, so maybe you should just pay for the parking...

Venice: I like to park in the neighborhood east of Main St. and north of the big roundabout with weird art in the middle. You can walk or skate a couple blocks and get to the beach, but mind the traffic! Even two blocks away, though, street parking can be sparse. You may have to loop around a few times, or just bite the bullet and pay to park – it can be worth it if the alternative is wasting 20 minutes of surf-time finding parking!

Santa Monica: There is a great little lot at Bay St. and Ocean Way. If you get there before 8:00AM, parking is free (That is also about the only time the waves are really decent here anyway). Pay attention to street cleaning signs though! They are plentiful, confusing, and perhaps even contradictory...

Hermosa Beach: My favorite spot in Hermosa is right at the end of it, just before the Redondo Beach Pier starts. (That's almost like saying, "My favorite part of the movie was when it was over.") Actually, I learned years later that this break is indeed part of Redondo Beach, but I'm going to leave it as Hermosa because you can walk to the pier from here. Take Herondo to the end and go left. There is a metered lot on the right that *sometimes* has parking. If not, there is another lot ahead on the left that used to be $1 per hour to park, and you even slipped it in a little box so if you went over by a few (twenty) minutes, you likely wouldn't get ticketed. This spot got pretty popular, however, and on the right swell it can get huge and hollow here, ripe for barrels. As a result, you now have to pay sometimes as much as $6 per hour to park here! It isn't always that much though, and you pretty much pull right up to the beach, so it's worth a shot to check it out. The alternative is to make friends with someone who lives in the apartments right next to it and park in their visitor spots, which are often open!

Redondo Beach/RAT Beach: There is free parking on the street on Esplanade, just south of Veteran's Park. Find your way down to the jetty and hope there is something good to ride. If you go down to RAT (Right After Torrance), there are big lots you can pay to park in, or sometimes find parking in the neighborhood up top. (Shout-out to my friend and skate team manager Shawn who also runs a skate clothing brand called Rat Beach Style. Check them out online and tell them Rick sent you!)

DISCLAIMER: (Not the name of a beach.) Infrastructure in Los Angeles changes faster than a fresh dredging will ruin your spot, so please don't write me to complain that what I wrote here isn't true anymore. I mean, you *can* write me, and if I release an updated edition, I will correct the mistakes. Just be nice when you do it, okay?

THE WHALE

SOMETIMES WHEN YOU ARE sitting out on the big blue Pacific, gazing at a horizon that seems to stretch forever, you cannot help but feel kind of small. But then again, you are in it. You're sitting waist deep in that mysterious mammoth of an ocean, and as you bob up and down with the riffs of energy that flow through its liquid limbs you somehow become one with it. Even if it's just for the few moments when your mind stretches out and your spirit goes down, past your body and its buoyancy, through the board to connect with that very same energy that lifts and pulls you. There was a time when I felt this connection more than any other. It was at Dockweiler. And it was when I saw…The Whale.

I was having a quick afternoon surf session on a Saturday or Sunday after the wind blew out any good waves that might have been possible, which is probably why I was the only one out. The sun was high, but past its zenith. The air was warm, and as you looked out over the ocean or to the north towards Santa Monica, you could see the white haze of marine layer hindering visibility. Being a small day, I likely had lots of time between sets. Sitting. Waiting. Wishing. Maybe even singing a line or two from one of my favorite musicians, though likely out of context. Anyway, I remember scanning the horizon for nothing – which always surprises you when you actually do see something – and that is when I noticed what looked like the foamy spray of a huge fountain way out in the distance.

Was that a whale? I thought, and then quickly dismissed the idea. I was about thirty yards offshore, far too close to the beach to see anything as massive as a whale. Still, I kept my eyes out, just in case I was right. And then it happened again – the spout stretched forth from the water like a quick spray from a fire hose. *Yes, that was a whale! Had to be!* Or...maybe it was just a really big bird diving for food. Which was more likely? I'm not sure. But I did see *something...*

And then it happened, the truly amazing part. It leapt out the water! Washington Mutual-style! I had confirmation that I, in fact, was sharing the water with a whale.

"Of course you're sharing the ocean with a whale," I am sure you're saying to yourself, "The Pacific is *full* of whales." Yes, but have you ever been *in* the water and then *saw* one? It's different (I promise). It takes that connectivity to a whole new level. Silly as it may sound, and as far off as the whale likely was (at least a few hundred yards), I saw it leap out of the water, the very same hydrogen-oxygen mixture that I was floating in myself. It may have even been close enough for the trickles of its wake to lap against my wetsuit as I waited for more jumps...to no avail. The whale was one-and-done as they say, but the memory of what I saw was burned into the record books of my mind with a hot-iron sear.

The majesty of such a large creature exposing itself from the water below created in me a sense of both awe and fear. If it had been any closer, I am not sure what I would have done – even a dolphin swimming by kind of freaks me out – but at the same time I felt so privileged to have seen the act, and much more to have shared the same space with such an amazing and massive creature.

The whole thing brings to mind what "fear of the LORD" means. Psalm 111:10 reads, *"The fear of the LORD is the beginning of wisdom; all who follow his precepts have good understanding. To him belongs eternal praise."* Many people struggle with the idea of fearing God, because how can we fear someone we love? I believe a good way to think of it is a reverential awe that reminds you of your place in the whole history of humanity on this big rock. Read the end of the book of Job – when the reader is reminded of how little we are and how big God is – it is no wonder why *that* concept is the beginning of wisdom. And then to think that God reveals anything to us, cares for us, has an interest in us, loves us – *died* for us. Well, that is a picture that demands response.

After the splash disappeared and I no longer saw any more activity, I looked to my right and left and saw no one. The beach was empty. I was the only one who got to experience this sight, which made it all the more meaningful. It was as if God commanded the mighty creature to put on a show just for me, which, in my experience, is just how God is. Even if it was just a coincidence, I will never forget the day I saw the whale at Dockweiler, and the lasting connection I felt to the ocean I once called home.

I wrote this song while thinking about my wife one day in our humble Redondo Beach apartment. She has blue eyes, which is something I never really sought out, but later grew to love. It felt similar to my love for the ocean, which grew over time, and is the spot where this song was born.

OCEAN EYES

I see the ocean in your eyes
Underneath the bright blue skies
And soon I'd find out
I never knew
Find the horizon
And I'd see you

I always searched for eyes of earth
A deeper brown, a darker dirt
But soon I'd find out
I never knew
When I was looking all around
God gave me you

I guess it figures that I'd find
A love that's true
In your love deep as the ocean
In your eyes of ocean blue

I looked for love in fields of green
Wooded valleys and city streets
And then I found out
I never knew
That there was love in all those
   places
But not you

I guess it figures that I'd find
A love that's true
In your love deep as the ocean
In your eyes of ocean blue

I guess it figures that the
Place I love to be
Can be found in your ocean eyes
Every time you're next to me

There is a romance that's of old
Love in legends and stories told
I'd later find out
I never knew
The love I see in your ocean eyes
Proves them all true

I used to love the mountains most
Until I fell hard for the coast
And then I found out
Now I know
Just like my love for your blue eyes
The best love grows

And then I found out
Now I know
Just like my love for your ocean eyes
The best love grows

DUCK DIVING

I REMEMBER THE FIRST time I ever rode the face of a wave. The image of the nose of my board splitting the water like an overcooked sausage on a hot grill is seared into my mind. The feeling afterward as I tried to explain the stoke to my dad and friend Nathan, who I was surfing with, is also there, as I picture their somewhat blank stares. They were both far more seasoned surfers than me and knew exactly what I was feeling; but also had that look you give a toddler when she tells you she just learned how to do a cartwheel, when it's actually just putting her head on the ground and a foot in the air, expecting you to celebrate as emphatically as she is. You do, of course, but you know that hers was a shadow of a true cartwheel and her capabilities will only grow with age. She has only scratched the surface. It was the same look, because they both knew I had just experienced a tiny milestone in my journey of riding that would go so, so much farther.

I also remember the paddle out on that session at the Folly Beach Pier. It was tough. I was far from in "surfing shape," having only recently begun a reawakened interest in surfing after the afore-mentioned board had hit me on the head in my younger years. As the waves pounded me back to shore, like guards protecting the walls of a sacred castle, I questioned whether I would ever make it out on what felt like a hundred-mile paddle. Not wanting to appear weak before my father and friend was likely my main motivation for not giving up that day, and the reward was well worth it. Had I known about a magical little thing called a "duck dive" on that session, however, it would have saved me a little time. Nathan was the first one to ever tell me about the technique, but sadly, it would be about another decade or so before I could even successfully perform one. Slow learner, remember?

Duck diving is when you thrust the board down underwater, followed by your body, to try and go below an oncoming wave. It is crucial to paddling out, and therefore crucial to successful surfing. In Charleston, the break is usually about thirty yards off the beach, so if you get lucky, you can sometimes avoid duck diving. In California, however, the break can be a hundred yards at many breaks, so if you want to be any kind of successful, or even comfortable, surfing in SoCal, you better start practicing these little quackers!

During my first season of surfing Santa Monica with Tyler, I remember a particularly huge day when neither one of us made it to the break. Daunted, we fought and fought until it became apparent that, even if we had been able to make it out, the waves were crashing with too much force and all at once (a closeout), that riding one would have been futile, particularly for such beginners. Not too long after, I followed Justin to his favorite spot at El Porto, where the paddle out proved equally painful. With a borrowed wetsuit I aimlessly pointed my nose seaward and never made it past the whitewater. The picture below shows me smiling, but look closer and you might see the inner turmoil of shameful defeat that I was really feeling.

Defeat on a sunny day. (Photo by Katie Bickerstaff)

It took about three or four years before I could even confidently perform a duck dive. More experienced friends would give me tips on how to do it, but it just never seemed to work – my board wouldn't go underwater enough and I would inevitably get clobbered. Then, a particularly messy session at Huntington Beach with my brother-from-another-mother Robb Leo Gilligan III, shed some light on the missing element: my feet.

HB has a notoriously long paddle out, and while we were wrestling with white water, we noticed other guys were using their feet to push the board down, and then diving headfirst after it, coming up successfully on the other side. Sure enough, employing this technique proved useful. Another couple years of practicing on all those big California days, and I was eventually pretty good at it.

I can't emphasize enough how much learning to duck dive will change your surfing. You can make it out to the break without being completely exhausted (most of the time). Big waves lose their intimidation as you are confident you can make it under them (most of the time). You can surf longer and better (most of the time). So basically, most of the time you will have more fun!

But then there are those days when even a few good duck dives won't help you from making it out. The water simply won't allow it. These are days when you start to wonder why you even paddle out. They test your resolve and your capacity to see the bright side of a dark looming wave. Positivity (and oxygen) runs thin as waves get thick and hold you under. This is when fear sets in, and this is what the next season of my surfing tenure was unfortunately marked by.

PART THREE
FEAR

SURFING AND FEAR

IT WAS A RAINY day after Thanksgiving, and a friend had tipped me off to an incoming swell that would hit the South Bay of Los Angeles. I didn't expect much, though, as Dockweiler (which counts as the north end of South Bay, though only barely) is rarely gigantic, but surfing sounded better than Black Friday shopping, so I decided to head out.

Apparently, my fear of water is greater than my fear of people's opinions, because I ended up grabbing my sister's NSP (a mass-produced, flowered epoxy board with a purple butterfly in the middle...I liked to call it the Butterfly Racer) for this seemingly less-than-epic surf session. It was wider than my short board, which helped in smaller waves, but still responsive enough to do some carving with a thruster fin setup. I would not advise you to go out and buy one by any means, but I remember being surprised at how much fun I had on this thing.

Riding the Butterfly Racer at Trestles...don't judge me.
(Photo by Rochelle LeHeux)

When I got to the spot, I was surprised to find a guy handily dropping in on a head-high left – a rare sight at Docks. I watched one more solid set come through while scoping for a good paddle-out spot and headed into the water.

This beach escapism quickly became an amazing session: big lefts, hardly anyone on the water (save Mitchel and Rochelle, who joined me), mist off the white caps and a little rain. The weather, more than anything, is what made it memorable. Rarely does it rain in Southern California, which perhaps adds to the mystic of surfing in it. The sky mimicked a stone as I watched waves roll past, the saltwater stinging my eyes in a way that felt like salve. After a good hour or so, Mitchel and I decided to paddle over towards a jetty (or groin, as Mitchel likes to correct me) where some folks looked like they were getting nice big right-handers, breaking way past where they usually did. And this is when the fear set in...

I later learned that this was a legendary swell that we were so humbly receiving. If you look up Thanksgiving surfing in 2013, you will see videos of peeling rights at El Porto, with guys getting barreled in waves that resemble Bali perfection. I also later learned that Russell had almost drowned the day before, naïvely paddling into fifteen-foot waves while still remaining very much a novice. He survived to tell the tale, though, and now rides such waves with ease.

In the new spot by the groin (you're welcome, Mitchel), we were sitting on beautiful glassy water, again farther out than is usual for Dockweiler, when I saw a set approaching. The water got shallow beneath me as the oncoming wave sucked the ocean right up into its lofty hallows. As I examined the growing bulge of water that approached me, I literally thought, *This could be the biggest wave of my life.* I paddled, asking myself whether I could survive it: *Will it close out on me? I hate dropping in on steep closeouts. If I paddle for this, I'm just going to go over the falls. Do I really want to almost drown right now?*

Those were the thoughts that ran through my head as I paddled and, as fear won over, pulled out. I then watched the wave move past me like a herd of buffalo to where Mitchel caught it. I can't remember how long he rode it, or if it closed out on him, but what I do remember is that I felt like less of a man at that moment.

Courage is a big part of surfing. "Normal" people don't paddle out into walls of water twice their size for nothing but the thrill of riding them. It takes a lot of gusto to face something bigger than yourself, but it is a trait we as humans value greatly – David and Goliath, Harry Potter and Voldemort, Laird Hamilton and Every Big Wave Ever. We all have our giants, and we each deal with them in our own way. For some this is just coming to terms with sharing the same space as the Men in the Gray Suits (sharks). Others are simply trying to stand up on a board. Still others are riding the heaviest waves in the world, with eight-story-buildings' worth of water collapsing behind them. All take courage, and all are usually well-worth the risk.

For me, this will forever be the "wave that got away." Whether or not it would have been a ride worthy of that title, I'll never know. But what I do know is this: a life lived in fear is a life lived in bondage, and sometimes the only way to recognize that is through missed opportunities and missed waves. What you do with that knowledge, however, is the real test of courage.

> *"God is our refuge and strength,*
> *an ever-present help in trouble.*
> *Therefore we will not fear, though the earth give way*
> *and the mountains fall into the heart of the sea,*
> *though its waters roar and foam*
> *and the mountains quake with their surging." (Psalm 46:1-3)*

> *"For the Spirit God gave us does not make us timid, but gives us power, love and self-discipline." (2 Timothy 1:7)*

Along with fear of things bigger than yourself comes awe, respect and maybe even love. If you hang out with surfers, you will likely find that many are quite spiritual, and I think this regular immersion into oceans and their power and majesty is one of the reasons. Way back in high school I wrote the music to this song, but could never quite land on good lyrics. Just this last year, however, I got a request for a "surf rock" song, and this one came to mind. I knew I wanted it to be worshipful as well as fun, and here is what resulted.

FOREVER FLOW

Hot sand under my feet
Eyes open and hoping to meet
The One who's done and running
It all
Horizon spread out wide
Bright sun shining its light over a
Blue ocean sparkling eyes like
A call

And all I see
Around me
Is beckoning
Us all

When I lift my eyes
To the skies to say, "Hello"
I see everything but me
And finally I know
As I walk this world so wide
I've got a well inside
A source of life that
Forever flows

Green grass under my feet
Barefoot and ready to greet
The wind blowing its way through
the trees
Like a song
Hands up (up!), up in the sky
Feet down (down!), side by side
Voice out (shout!) ready to answer
That call

And all I see
Around me
Is beckoning
A song

When I lift my eyes
To the sky and say, "Hello"
I see everything but me
And finally I know
As I walk this world so wide
I've got a well inside
A source of life that
Forever flows

Let's go!

THE FEAR OF MISSING OUT

RUSSELL SENT ME A picture of the surf report (seven to nine feet at El Porto) early one week with the caption, "Too bad we're at work…" Too bad indeed…a big WNW swell had been hitting Los Angeles all week, but I was likely to miss it because the sun came up as I was on my way to work, and went down before I got home. To make matters worse, my car broke down the week before, and so the bus had doubled my commute time, making an early evening surf session impossible. It was like a tragic country song written only for surfers: *"Hello walls…of water."*

The swell was weakening as the week went by, so by the time Saturday hit, I would have missed the best parts. So, what does one do in a crisis such as this? I had narrowed it down to a few logical options:

- Quit your job and go surfing
- Call in "sick" and go surfing
- Miss the swell

The first option sounded pretty appealing, but not so practical. Number two was against my code of ethics. So that left option three – and with it came two sub-options: complain or deal with it.

And so, I sat at my desk, looking out the window as the wind gently pushed the palm branches outside, imagining those same trees were beachfront and that I was there, catching what could have been the best waves of my life. But would they have really been the best waves of my life? Maybe. They could also have ended up being big ugly close-outs that were next-to-impossible to drop in on. I'll never know, and that is where the anxiety lies – missing out on unknown potential.

Fear of missing out is an epidemic running rampant these days (usually tied to social media in some way or another), but surfers have been feeling this for decades, as the responsibilities of life often don't line up with nature's seemingly random gifts. Even when we're on the water, arguments break out because other surfers snake (steal) waves, or beachgoers get in the way. Or maybe you get mad because you slipped on that last drop in and you swear it was going to be the best wave of the day, grumbling as you paddle in for more wax and hoping for a second chance.

Expectation and imagined potential are the enemies here. I can sit at my desk and picture perfect barrels over my head, when in reality it's probably as closed as Chick-Fil-A on Sundays. I can look at a wave and imagine myself hitting every corner, spraying beautiful ocean mist over the applauding onlookers...but we all know that's not happening. As a dreamer, I am not one to preach realistic expectations in life, but avoiding regret in the water (and in life) involves a healthy balance between optimism and reality. The other key to fighting FOMO is being happy where you are at (aka - contentment). After all, if you're stuck dwelling on missed opportunities, you won't be living optimally in the moment.

Take delight…even on a crappy day! (Photo by Katie Bickerstaff)

Yeah, you might miss the peak part of the swell, but maybe you'll catch some nice waves on Saturday…and it might be huge, or it could be a bust. But as the theme of this book is slowly becoming, "It's always nice to get out on the water." The saying rings true, and that should be enough.

"Take delight in the LORD,
And He will give you the desires of your heart.
Commit your way to the LORD;
Trust in Him and He will do this:
He will make your righteous reward shine like the dawn,
Your vindication like the noonday sun.
Be still before the LORD
And wait patiently for Him" (Psalm 37:4-7a)

I wrote a song while sitting at the same desk mentioned in this piece, watching those lofty palm trees sway on a different dreamy afternoon, again wishing I was outside. Take a look at the lyrics and take a listen if you have the album. If you don't…you might be missing out. (Don't fear though! It's available somewhere!)

BULLY (OFFICE SPACE)

*There's a window at my office
And the sun shines on everything
  but me
And the trees are all shaking
Being bullied gently by the breeze
And I want to be a part of it
But I've got five more hours till
  I'm free
I'm hoping that the sun stays up
And the breeze wants to bully me*

*It's fall in my spirit, winter in my
  soul
Spring in my heart and summer
  in my bones
And all of these feelings,
  misguided and misplaced
Longing for a place to run, but
  finding only office space*

*Half of all the blinds are shut
And the lights are low
  surrounding my cube
It's like a gentle bully
Punch the clock and punch my
  heart too*

*I know I sound ungrateful
I thank God for means to provide
But sometimes I'm just wishin'
  that my
Provision was a position outside*

*It feels like the worlds largest fish
  bowl
Open outside, but within it's just
  full
Of an endless sea of monotony
And bureaucracy, but hey, they
  pay me*

And that's what I need
Like a horseradish seed
The taste is just bitter so
It must be good for me
But I've got to believe
There's more there for me
Than the corporate bully

But comfort is never free...
Maybe comfort isn't for me.

It's fall in my spirit, winter in my
*   soul*
Spring in my heart and summer
*   in my bones*
And all of these feelings,
*   misguided and misplaced*
Longing for a place to run, but
*   finding only office space*

TWENTY-TWO MILES

IT WAS THE WINTER of 2013. My wife and I were tired of living on the east side of Los Angeles, not because it was bad (truly, I loved it), but because it was just too far from the beach...twenty-two miles to be exact. Now I know some of you must be reading this and thinking, *Twenty-two miles?! I live twenty-two-hundred miles from the beach! Stop complaining!* But when you dwell in Los Angeles, twenty-two miles is usually a solid hour in traffic; and when you live in a coastal town, you might as well *live* coastal, right?!

We found a great little duplex to rent literally a mile-and-a-half from the beach, and a half-a-block away from two of our best friends, Aaron and Ashley. Our place had a yard, room to garden, and a shared garage where we kept our drum set and a few surfboards hanging from the rafters. It really was everything Southern California dreams are made of...at least to us.

Author, considering the quiver in our duplex garage. (Photo by tripod)

Being relatively new to the area, I wanted to check out the closest break to us, which was Playa. I paddled out one Saturday into pretty fair waves with no one else in sight. As I surfed, I wondered, *Why is no one else out here? These waves aren't bad.* Just about then, I saw what looked like a human head with silver hair pop out of the water and then go back down. An old guy swimming, I figured, and kept an eye on the spot to see if he came up...

He didn't.

I waited a while and never saw a thing. *Okay, that's kind of freaky*, I thought. It didn't look like a seal with the gray hair, but maybe it was just the way the sun was hitting its wet fur. Either way, I went home and researched the spot a bit – it sits at the mouth of Ballona Creek, which is a man-made river that runs through Los Angeles and dumps into the ocean. The problem with surfing here is obvious – garbage, city-muck, and who-knows-what floating out from this "river," which despite being disgusting also attract seals...and sharks. Needless to say, that was the last time I ever surfed there.

However, just a couple jetties up is what I consider the border of Dockweiler (even though it is really part of Playa Vista). There is a restroom building right at the junction of Napoleon St. and Vista Del Mar, where a broken-down dock marks what was one of my favorite surf spots in Los Angeles. There is plenty of parking, without the crowds that show up for Dockweiler's firepits just a few jetties south. It is quiet, and the facilities are encircled by palm trees with the space filled in by seemingly misplaced, but beautifully lush, grass – it is pretty much the Oasis of Los Angeles. You can also ride your bike on the Marvin Braude Bike Trail (also known as The Strand) from Santa Monica, through here and all the way down to RAT Beach. It is truly the kind of thing normal peoples' California dreams are made of.

The Oasis of LA at Lifeguard Tower 49 (Photo by author)

I had surfed a few small days here before my first real memorable session. Mitchel and I had decided to surf, not checking the report from what I can remember (a bad habit of ours). Well, when we pulled up with our wives it was huge. So big that this was the first time I remember being really scared paddling out. It was pretty early in our surfing "career," and the waves were overhead and breaking left immediately in front of the broken-down pier, complete with lots of rocks and rusty pillars to impale yourself on. You had to catch them literally *right* in front of the pier, and if you slipped on the drop in or went over the falls, you were going to wish you had brought a helmet. Those that made the drop found themselves in a steep hollow wave that would barrel on the most fortunate of rides.

Mitchel and I, green as we were, sat on the outside for a long time before getting the courage to enter the lineup. We tried to catch a few straggling lefts at the far edge to build our confidence, with some success. I also remember there was a body boarder who looked like Anthony Kiedis from the Red Hot Chili Peppers. There is actually a watchful little crew that surfs here regularly (Anthony Kiedis isn't one of them), which is odd because most days it is about as flat and dumpy as Los Angeles can get. However, on the right swell, this spot really shines, left or right. At a date later than that first paddle out (and during another season when I was better at surfing), I caught head-high rights that went long and steep. I watched guys bust airs out of these same waves and even saw the occasional "Russell Barrel" (When the water just covers over your head, not your whole body... Does it count? Russell says it does!).

As I wrote earlier, most folks in this area head south to El Porto to get their waves, but if you are patient and aware, you can certainly score at Playa, minus the crowds and plus free parking. In my mind, it is really an extension of Dockweiler, which could be just another reason why I love it so much. However you categorize it, this is a premier spot in Los Angeles if you are willing to wait, and so I highly recommend checking it out. Do it before Silicon Beach takes over though and starts installing iPad-charging stations on the sand. That's the day I go vigilante...keep reading to see why.

SURFING AND TECHNOLOGY

I HAVE A LOVE-HATE relationship with technology. Actually, *like*-hate relationship is a better way of putting it. I'm that guy who gives people dirty looks when they're on their phone amongst friends, or appreciates asking strangers for directions instead of using a navigation app. I still buy CDs because I like having a physical backup of music, and I only own a tablet because my friend Jason gave me one.

Still, I am not too proud to admit that technology has its advantages, even applied to something as natural as surfing. So here are some technological advances that, to me, seem to enhance the sport we love.

Surf Report

When I was growing up you would call the Ocean Surf Shop hotline for Folly Beach, SC to hear a recording of how the waves were that morning. It was always busy, so you had to call several times to hear it, and it was only done once or twice a day, so the accuracy was questionable. Now we have Surfline, which has live cameras from all over the world, saving surfers countless hours of time and disappointment in avoiding flat days.

Waves » Waist to stomach.	**WIND** » NW @ 10-15
SURF CONDITIONS » Side-shore, drifty, semi-clean.	**TIDES** » L: 12:52 p.m. / H: 7:08 p.m.
	WEATHER » 38°, with a biting wind.
FUN FACTOR »	**DANGERS** » Cold and rain.
	TRAFFIC » None.
WATER TEMPERATURE » 49°	**PARKING** » Plenty.
CURRENT NOAA FOLLY BUOY READINGS »	
SHARE THIS REPORT »	

Ocean Surf Shop's "Fun Factor": a staple of Folly.
(Photo courtesy of oceansurfshop.com)

Artificial Wave

The artificial wave is a growing trend, and I have to say I can't wait for it to become widespread. I don't know when that will happen, but with The Kelly Slater Wave Company, Wave Garden, and Surf Snowdonia, maybe rich folks wanting a new hobby in Kansas will start building. The good thing about these waves is that everyone knows they will never, ever replace surfing a natural break. And so you can surf here when it is flat or to build some skills, and no one is going to say, "Yeah, but it isn't *real* surfing." Of course it's not real surfing! But after a few days there, you can bet you'll enjoy a whole lot more "real" surfing, because you'll be that much better.

Look at the videos of it – even pros look like their thighs are melting after riding one of these things! It is unnatural to surf a wave for that long (minute*s*...*plural*!), and so we're not used to it; but isn't that the dream? Long rides, consistent barrels, clean faces. Imagine how good you would be if you had this in your hometown! And there is still a benefit for all the pure naturalists out there: something like this would certainly clear the lineup a bit at your local break!

I must admit that, deep down, I have a *little* push back against things like this. It just seems a little *too* perfect, and what in life is truly perfect? But even if these popped up in every mildly populated city in the world, surfing at beaches would never go away; just as an abundance of skate parks doesn't seem to deter street skating. There is something about finding your own way on a board that is too magical to fabricate.

Board Innovation

We don't have flying cars yet, but we do have jet-propelled surfboards! The WaveJet started it and went out of business, but there are currently several other jet-propelled surfboard companies out there. The benefit is being able to paddle out three-to-four times faster, as well as catch huge waves without a tow-in. These also come in handy after a long surf session and your body wants to give out, even though the waves continue pumping. But then the challenge becomes how to avoid looking like the laziest surfer on the planet riding one of these...

Similar (and on some models, much the same) are foil boards, which have a hydrofoil that extends below the surface of the water, while you rise above on your board, the two attached by a thin rail that cuts through the water. This helps foil surfers go faster, but also avoid choppy water since the board is connected to the foil by the much thinner piece. I first saw one of these ridden by Laird Hamilton in the 2003 film Step Into Liquid. It only took about twenty years for me to see these in the lineup, but they show up every now and then. Guys cruise on them through waves and then up and out and back to the top of the lineup, but they really have to pump to get it going, from what I've seen. Still, it saves a lot of energy and is certainly a longer ride; you just have to get used to everyone gawking at you while you shred (and hopefully not wipe out).

A little less high tech are the assortment of advancements in board materials available today. From new types of foam to epoxies, you can now get a lighter, more buoyant board than ever before. I am constantly amazed at the guys riding tiny "potato chip boards" (as my dad calls them) and still managing to get in on small waves. It's part skill, sometimes mixed with a little bit of a size disadvantage (or advantage in this sense), but I know super-light epoxy is helping some too.

My friend Nelson is really into fin technology. I never dove too much into this, outside of the now standard FCS removable fins, but he swears it makes a difference to try out all sorts of types of fins for your boards. To me, there's something about riding what you have and making it work that's rugged, maybe even American; but he's a better surfer than me so maybe I am just cheap and stupid.

Wetsuits and Boardshorts

Imagine being a surfer in the yonder-days, enjoying the beach on a crisp winter afternoon, watching beautiful waves break in front of you. But if you paddled out in that water for more than twenty minutes, you'd have borderline hypothermia. I'm sure it happened – you can't keep a surfer out of the water – but thank God neoprene was invented and now we can surf the planet from top to bottom, year-round (there is a great film that takes place when this happened called *Drift*, that I recommend for both entertainment and a little surf history). As innovation progresses I have been hearing about heated wetsuits, and even suits that protect you from sharks! (I'm on board for that one.)

I always thought board shorts were a simple thing, but more and more I am seeing changes in materials and design so you can get the most out of your surfing. For instance, Hurley makes shorts with a breathable waistband and material that stretches and moves with you, allegedly increasing your maneuverability and performance. So salute your shorts – they're making a difference!

So there is the good/bad list, depending on your point of view. Whether you are riding a board you found in some back alley of Venice Beach, or a $3,000 custom-shaped egg, the mystical allure of surfing is still there. If you have the money, why not spend it on all this new-age technology? Or maybe you could dump it into a surf trip to Fiji instead…remember, experience will make you a better person than stuff, and your character is all you can take with you in the end.

"Do not store up for yourselves treasures on earth, where moths and vermin destroy, and where thieves break in and steal. But store up for yourselves treasures in heaven, where moths and vermin do not destroy, and where thieves do not break in and steal. For where your treasure is, there your heart will be also." (Matthew 6:19-21)

Looking to invest in this incredible sport? Here are some of my favorite places to buy surf equipment in Los Angeles:

- Soul Performance: I love this shop! Mark is the owner and has been shaping boards in the South Bay of Los Angeles for decades under the brand Brög Surfboards. It's the kind of shop you can go into and hang out for a while, which is always the best kind.
- ET Surf: Just east of the PCH, this shop is a staple of the beach cities action sports community. They have everything

you need from surf to skate to snowboard, as well as ample parking and close proximity to the beach. I once saw Wee Man (of *Jackass* fame) here, which lets you know that it is legit!

- Dive and Surf: This is the big shop in the South Bay. Located just between Hermosa and Redondo, you can grab some wax here on your way to surf RAT, or stop in and chat with one of the local workers. I'm not much of a diver, but given the title, I think they have that covered as well. They also have a year-round clearance shop in an adjoining building that I'm a big fan of.

- Jack's Surf Shop: These are all over Southern California, and are a pretty decent shop. They have killer deals on wetsuits around late-winter/early-spring, so check them out to snag a suit and surf all year long.

- Action Watersports: At the southernmost end of Venice was once my favorite shop north of South Bay. They had amazing deals on used boards, as well as plenty of great new gear, along with snowboarding equipment. They also had a cool decorative fiberglass wave built out front that will inspire you to surf whenever you drive by. May she Rest in Peace...

Note: There are a ton more...Rider Shack, Mollusk, Val Surf. But the ones above are this author's personal recommendations.

HUMILITY - PRIDE COMES
BEFORE A WIPEOUT

IT IS WRITTEN THAT pride comes before a fall (Proverbs 16:18). But the Bible doesn't mention anything about the washing machine tumult *after* the fall, followed by gasping for air, a snapped leash, and a long swim in. The winter of 2013-2014 was a big one for me in Southern California, with waves in the twenty-plus-foot range at some breaks. But rather than story after story of triumphant waves ridden into glory, most of what I encountered was a big fat slap of humility. Surfing is a progression, and so calling a wave "big" can be a relative thing. That being said, I spent that winter paddling into progressively bigger surf, and as I had been thrashed and also conquered, my sense of what I could handle grew. And as it grew, I must admit that a little pride crept up into my waterlogged brain...

February 2014: Massive swell coming through. My friends and I shared bloated surf reports through texts and social media leading up to the weekend, excited for the potential glory ahead. But deep down, a nagging worry was there in the pit of my stomach asking if I could handle it.

Of course I could handle it…right?

The big day came and, after checking out a couple of unsurfable spots (huge closeouts on shallow sand), we back-tracked to Malibu pier, where some other guys looked like they were having a good time. We suited up and paddled out, only to immediately get swept into a current and carried down into a cove and back to shore. Thus the humility began. This happened three more times as I would head for the break, only to get carried away and pounded by the ten-foot waves. All the while I was watching guys shred beautiful right-handers, snapping the tops of overhead sets and then paddling back for more like it was their morning warm-up.

After the fourth thwarted attempt, I decided I wouldn't be kept down and, hitting a rare lull between sets, I made it out. The current was still bad here, and you pretty much had to maintain some degree of swimming-motion just to stay in position. I tried to rest for a quick minute, which brought me to the outside corner of the sets – a nice place to wait for some lesser wave to come my way (which was fine with me at this point). Well, the wave came sooner than I expected, and so I paddled and caught it, but that's when things get as hazy as a West Coast IPA…

To this day, I'm still not sure exactly what happened, except that I was soon falling down a steep drop on an eight-to-ten-foot wave with no board under my feet. I hit the water and found myself in the washing machine – a recently frequent friend of mine. I maintained calm and made it out, catching a breath before the next wave hit. Eventually, I surfaced again and then reached for my leash, hoping to save this wasted set; or maybe just make it out alive. To no avail -- my leash was gone! I looked ahead to find my board being tossed and carried off to shore; my St. Bernard rescue dog swept away by an avalanche.

I backstroked my way in while praying to not die – after all, I had a daughter on the way and I wanted to be there for that! God must have heard because after a little swim I found my board literally parked about halfway in, caught on some kelp (which never happens). When I finally hit the shore, I didn't go back. For the record, my friends didn't do much better than me, so we all chalked it up to experience and a little extra duck-diving practice, and headed to Jack in the Box across the street for some self-indulgent fast food.

Fast-forward a few days and Russell tells me he went out again, catching more of the big swell, but wasn't able to make it to the break. *Really Russell? You couldn't even make it out?* I haughtily thought to myself. *What a lamewad...*(Yes, my thoughts are akin to a ten-year-old from 1993.) And that is when it happened, the swift slap of humility's palm...

A few days later I pulled up to what is normally a fairly docile beach (can you guess the spot?), but the waves were breaking thirty yards past their normal area in huge sets. Fear set in. My breathing quickened. My heart raced as I watched the waves while approaching the beach, thinking to myself, *Your daughter is due next week, Rick. Don't die.* (My mind goes straight to mortality when surfing, doesn't it?)

The middle waves were heavy closeouts, and so I made it my goal to paddle out to the huge sets in the back. I looked for my spot, eventually finding a little lull, and went for it. I got handily punched by some incredibly handsome whitewash as I watched the only other surfer out catch a beautiful right and ride it with style. Eventually, I made it pretty far before I realized I didn't put nearly enough wax on my board, because I was sliding all over the place – amateur mistake. So I went back in without catching a single wave and waxed up.

Try #2: More of the same – pounding and never-ending sets.

As soon as I thought I had made it out to the break, I peeked over the crest of the wave and one twice its size was crashing in front of me. I got a lot of duck-diving practice that day...a lot. Well, a man can only take so much, and I was hitting my limit. For some reason, I was also getting spooked paddling in the white after-wash of the larger waves: In my dramatic mind, this is the type of water sharks like to dwell in. So after biting my lip on a duck-dive-gone-wrong and feeling like a shark hit my foot (because they can smell blood up to a mile away, and apparently transport immediately to the source of said blood), I paddled in.

Defeated and dejected, scared and bleeding, I performed the walk of shame back to my backpack on the beach – all the while watching awesome waves roll in, one after the other. Soon the other surfer (he had all those waves to himself!) came in and told me about how wonderful the waves were at the break; so powerful, in fact, that he had broken one of his fins during the ride. I sheepishly told him I never made it past the break. "Oh," he said, with a little consolation in his voice, and nothing more. After he left, I stood there for a long time, watching the water and wondering if I should have paddled back out. I wanted to. I'm not one to quit easily. But the reasons to stop (fatigue, responsibilities back home, my bleeding lip and the "shark") kept popping up. So I left.

As I walked to my car, I decided that this would not be a defining moment in my life. I wouldn't be the guy who gives up after half-an-hour of paddling because he's tired. It was just an off day. A day counted as experience and a good workout. A day to be forgotten, save the lessons learned. A day where humility won, which isn't always such a bad thing.

If pride is the downfall of man, then surfers should run the world. We face nature daily, and even the most experienced riders get rocked sometimes. We know our place here, humbly accept it, and then push a little farther to see how much wiggle room there just might be. For some of us, that's riding mountains of water, and others, tiny mounds. But even the smallest of waves, on the wrong day at the wrong time, can bury you. This is the humility we must accept to ride on. Tread lightly in these waters, my friends, and take each wave with the gratitude of a humble man who knows each moment as a gift. For that is all it is.

And that is still enough.

A HUMBLE SURFER'S POLITICAL RANT

SURFERS COME IN PLENTY of packages. There are, of course, the typical beach bum surfer and the bro-dude surfer, seen in *Fast Times at Ridgemont High* (and every other movie with a surfer in it, ever). Though sensationalized, those guys are real! Case and point: the El Porto surfer who made famous the phrase, "Get pitted!" (Look it up.) But then sometimes you find business owners, accountants, airline workers and a whole host of other non-surfery folks who love to paddle out on a regular basis. I will never forget the Southern Baptist preacher I met who loved to hunt, fish, and play country/western music on his guitar. This same guy once told me he only lasted one week in high school football practice because the coach wouldn't let him surf. Go figure...

Anyway, I think you find this variety because a surfer's life is about balance – literally while on the board and figuratively while finding time to surf between family obligations, work meetings, and mowing the lawn; not to mention being able to do it *only* when nature cooperates. It makes sense that this life in balance can find itself landing in lots of different places with lots of different people. To segue into my little political rant, I think this idea of balance is why I had come to some sad conclusions about the 2016 race for the presidency, the year I started this book and certainly a year that will go down in political infamy.

My wife and I had missed most of the debates on both sides of the political spectrum (there are only two sides of course...) and so we spent a couple weeks catching up after the fact. What I found is that I kept gravitating towards the candidates who seemed somewhat moderate in what they said, were levelheaded and respectful in their demeanor and, for some reason, *extremely unpopular*. I was disheartened to see that these candidates, who kept throwing out comments that made a lot of sense, particularly in the realm of bridging gaps in politics to actually get things done, were largely overlooked. Literally placed at the fringes of the stages, these men were often excluded from questions, denied the responses they were due, and given significantly less time to stake their cases for the presidency. At the end of it, since we were catching up on things, I was sad to find many of them had already dropped out of the race due to said unpopularity.

What I want to write about here is how ridiculous it is that what could be the most logical candidates are the ones who are pushed out of the race because they just aren't very good for news. (This is where I point out the word "humble" in the title, because I am going to admit that my research on every candidate was fairly limited. My comments here are based mostly, though not entirely, on the debates.) People want a show and so the media brings it. For all the reasons above we are left missing the words of guys and gals who could be *really good* leaders, but because they don't embody a strict conservative or liberal platform (or maybe just don't *act* like they do), and aren't boisterous or argumentative, we may never hear from them again on this scale.

It is shameful that we only give our attention to those who cause the most noise. We are choosing leaders, not casting a movie. Objectively, wouldn't you want someone who is level-headed, respectful of his or her peers, not afraid to deviate from party lines every now and then – someone who is overall *balanced* – to make decisions that affect this country and the rest of the world? I know I do! But because that is not all that interesting, we will push the men and women who just might be the most qualified for the job to the side of the stage, regard their meager speaking time as an annoying formality, and microwave some popcorn until the next argument breaks out.

Yes, this was American politics in 2016... I don't know if any politicians surf, but if they do, I bet part of it is to escape from the circus. And I wouldn't blame them! But hey, maybe if they *all* surfed, things would be better. Parking at every beach would be free, renourishment would disappear, and the snaker of waves would be outlawed. But our world is far from perfect, isn't it? And so I guess we'll just have to wait for Jesus to come back and fix everything.

I am pretty sure he would be a surfer – he already knows how to walk on water, right?

"And I heard a loud voice from the throne saying, 'Look! God's dwelling place is now among the people, and He will dwell with them. They will be His people, and God Himself will be with them and be their God. He will wipe every tear from their eyes. There will be no more death or mourning or crying or pain, for the old order of things has passed away.'" (Revelation 21:3-4)

DON'T FEAR THE STANDOUT

HAVE YOU EVER BEEN sitting in the lineup and waiting for a set when, out of nowhere, a giant bulge of water comes at you like a miniature tsunami? You're in line where the break usually hits, but this is something different, breaking farther out and bigger – the head of a Kraken, a behemoth, a BROhemoth! And so you have to make a split-second decision to either paddle and beat the wave, diving through the only weak point of the beast, piercing its flabby shallows; or sit and hope to dodge its fists, duck diving a swarm of white water in a last ditch effort to make it out alive.

You choose the first option: Paddle! As fast as you can! The wave is growing, becoming darker, ready to double over. You're close, just a few more strokes away! The wave crests and you thrust your board down just in time to avoid taking it on the head. When you come up on the other side of a miracle, you look back and watch boards and heads pop up in a massive pool of sea foam and whitewater, gasping for air and hoping there isn't another one on the way...but there usually is. This is the story of a standout set, my friends, and knowing how to handle these is key for a successful surf session on a big day.

Oblivious to approaching dangers...turn around!
(Photo by Jinee Joung)

Handling standout sets is all about decision making: camp out deep and wait for the standout, or go back and catch a few, hoping the standout doesn't come. I've been on both sides and I'll tell you the results:

- **The good thing about waiting deep** is that you will be safe from rogue waves that clear the lineup, and you might even catch one if you're bold enough to ride a monster. You also may be able to take advantage of the aftermath and have some waves to yourself if the next set allows.
- **The bad part** is that you may end up waiting forever for these standouts and miss many regular sets in the process.
- **The good thing about staying shallow** is that you will catch the regular sets along with everyone else.

- **The bad part** is that you probably won't be in position to beat the standout and, like 2AM at the bar, will be cleared out along with everyone else.

A time when the standouts determined the day for me was during the infamous Hurricane Marie swell in 2014 (check out the next chapter for more). The standouts were rolling in at eight-to-ten-feet on our day, and with a lot of rocks hidden by the lineup, I did not want to miss a duck-dive and go over the falls on one of these. And so what I did was camp out *between* the regular lineup and standout set. I'd see a standout and paddle out, beating it, and then paddle back to just past the lineup to try and catch some of those. The problem with this strategy is that you miss a lot of waves because you're just *past* the regular break, and you're also living in constant fear that a standout is imminent; not to mention wearing yourself out paddling back and forth. It's kind of like a person who builds an underground shelter in fear of a zombie apocalypse, but then chooses to spend his nights and weekends there while also trying to live a normal life above ground – this person will inevitably live a halfway-life on both sides. (Weird analogy, I know...)

And so I learned an important lesson that day: don't fear the standout! I was so stressed paddling back and forth from the lineup to the standouts that I never caught a wave and didn't enjoy any of the epic swell I was receiving. In hindsight, I would have joined the lineup and caught some waves, and should a standout come...held my breath and tried to dive deep! It was a silly thing to live in fear between the lineups. A better approach would have been to take what waves I was given and hold on when the big ones came. Either that, or wait for the standout and get a few massively epic rides rather than several mildly epic rides...rider's choice.

Tips for Handling Standouts + a Little Inspiration

El Porto is notorious for standouts. You can find them anywhere, but something about this spot magnifies them. No joke – you'll be out on a three-to-five-foot day and suddenly an eight-foot wall of water will appear out of nowhere and wipe everyone out like a flyswatter. Everyone that is, except Russell, who is known for camping way, *way* out and waiting for the broheme. It's rewarding I'm sure – I've seen him ride some big waves – but this requires patience and foresight. You have to know the break well and understand what kind of swell is hitting. Then again, sometimes you just get a feeling that you need to go deeper, and you strike gold (see Intro).

If you're not as lucky as Russell, here are some tips, should you get caught in the washing machine of a standout gone wrong:

1. **Don't panic:** Surfing is dangerous and waves can be unpredictable. Still, staying calm will allow you to assess each situation with a clear mind, and prepare to escape accordingly. You will also save energy you would otherwise waste trying to fight a losing battle against the power of the sea...energy better used for swimming to safety after the wave has passed.

2. **Take a good breath:** If you see a standout approaching and know you're going to get mauled, take a deep breath and hold on! If I am paddling out on a particularly big day, sometimes I will take a lot of deep breaths to "stretch my lungs." Also remember that you can probably hold your breath longer than you think, so when your body is tempted to panic while underwater, don't!

3. **Hang on to your board:** Floating is always good, right? If you can hang on to your board through the washing machine, do it! A big giant floaty thing will inevitably pull you closer to the surface, which usually equals safety.

4. **Let the wave pass:** Don't go all Gandalf on the ocean...let it pass! Curl up and let the washing machine do what it wishes. You will be surprised at how quickly it passes, and also save energy for your ascension.

5. **Climb your leash (if you have to):** If you get so thrashed that you don't know which way is up, reach for your leash and start climbing. The board is floating and will lead you to safety.

6. **Prepare for the next wave:** You may have been thrashed by the first wave in a set of three colossi plowing through the lineup. Be ready for this by taking a deep breath first, and then checking for what might be ahead. If the shadow of another wave looms overhead, dive deep and go back to step three.

7. **Remember who made the oceans:** And know He is on your side! *"You answer us with awesome and righteous deeds, God our Savior, the hope of all the ends of the earth and of the farthest seas, who formed the mountains by your power, having armed yourself with strength, who stilled the roaring of the seas, the roaring of their waves, and the turmoil of the nations." (Psalm 65:5-7)*

HURRICANE MARIE

HURRICANES DON'T FREQUENT THE Pacific too often, but when they do, the West Coast can get hit with some epic swells. My first experience of this was Hurricane Marie in 2014. The stories coming in were unbelievable – twenty-to-thirty-foot waves at the Wedge. The same size breaking *past* the Malibu Pier. I chose not to hit the peak because of a healthy awareness of my surfing ability, but went out the day *after* to catch what I could.

Mitchel and I headed north in the brisk fall morning, hoping for some reef break rollers to sustain our pursuits. The waves were still crowded, which we expected, so we headed to the slightly less-accessible Point Dume. This spot is truly beautiful, a gem of Southern California. You drive past Zuma beach, where we stopped to watch a handful of guys attempt gnarly lefts that were barreling on this incredibly shallow beach break. Most of them got swallowed up, but I did see one make it out – an awesome sight. The bathroom stalls also don't have doors on them, so if you're a morning pooper and go out for an early session...be ready. (Just a little toilet tip.)

Anyway, you drive past the first point of Zuma and into the neighborhood just south of the spot. Climb a twisty hill and you will eventually see about eight parking spots in a row, where, if you're lucky enough to get one, you can take the dusty path to the cove known as Point Dume. From the top of the cliff you can see the waves coming in from a bird's eye view, which on this day looked like this:

An epic day at an epic location. (Photo by author)

These waves were large (they usually break before all that white-water you see), but we noticed guys were having trouble getting into them. When you visit this spot, you have to climb down a rusty staircase and then traverse some rocks to get to a point where you can paddle in. The trek can be a little dicey at high tide, but I have had nothing but fun days here, even when it was small. The waves break nice and smooth, sometimes barreling in a beautiful peeling motion like a banana split made at 120fps (I used to work at Baskin Robbins, so forgive my analogy). If you head through the large part of the cove, you will hit Little Dume, where Russell once met legendary surfer Laird Hamilton. He said the guy was surprisingly approachable, and surfed like he was Triton's grandson, which I suspect he just may be...

On this day we decided not to paddle into the lineup here for the aforementioned reason (plus it was a little crowded), and headed even farther north to Leo Carillo. Normally a bust (read "Supermoon Surfing" later to find out), we hit a rare eight-person lineup with head-high-plus sets. It was a beautiful day with great waves during an uncharacteristically *un*crowded session. As our day progressed, more folks did paddle out, but in the end I got some great rides, learned a few lessons, and faced a couple fears as well.

Hurricanes pretty much supply the entire surfing season for East Coasters. While others are planning their escape, surfers in the Carolinas are holding out as long as they can to catch the most waves before it gets too dangerous – and even after sometimes. It's good to know that the same thing can happen on the West Coast as well, which leads me to ask: could the West Coast be the Best Coast?

PART FOUR

FATHERHOOD

TRISHREDATHON

IT HAD HAPPENED BY accident a couple years prior...we had season passes to Mt. Baldy, the nearest ski mountain to LA, and decided to get one more day in as winter was ending and the little bit of spring Southern California gets was approaching with haste. I grew up riding the icy mountains of North Carolina, but after only two seasons of West Coast powder, had gotten pretty accustomed to it. That final day at Baldy was a throwback to my roots, which I quickly realized as I tossed myself off of a little kicker into what looked like soft snow...but wasn't.

A couple rides later I caught an edge and found myself sliding down the mountain with a tweaked shoulder. It wasn't long before we were exiting the tiny resort and heading back to town, counting Baldy as a bust. The silver lining was that it was the first hot day in Los Angeles in a while, and some friends were going to the beach. And that is when it hit me: I could feasibly snowboard, surf, and skateboard in one day. God bless California.

I managed all three that day, but only barely, as the skatepark was dark by the time I got to it and I was only able to do a few carves in the bowl to claim completion. And so, a couple of years later, and just one month before the birth of my first daughter, I decided to pursue the California Trifecta once again, this time for reals.

Korey, of the Starship Surfers, created this for the big day.

Months of planning led to a group of guys ready to ride the elements with me, though about a third dropped out the day before. Even though I had stayed up too late the night prior, and almost ate cereal with sour milk, I was hardly prepared me for hardships that lie ahead...

First up, surfing at Hammerland. It was a small, but glassy morning, which meant the Wavestorm was my board of choice. The rides were long and the camaraderie strong, and so after about two hours of fun in the water (as well as a bonus skimboarding session, so mark that a fourth sport), I went home for a snack and then a quick skate at the Culver City Skatepark.

This park has been one of my favorites for years, mostly due to the perfect pool and drainage ditch-style banks, along with a great kicker-to-flat. Unfortunately, the park was riddled with scooters and younger skaters, and so there was little room to shred. Still, I got in a few carves and a little street skating with my roller blading buddy Tim, before pressing on to the final sport, and the home-stretch.

It was a long ride to Mountain High, complete with good friends, a first Chick-Fil-A visit for one of the riders, and not-a-few punk songs. Needless to say, by the time we arrived I was nearly exhausted, but had come too far to turn back now with the sweet taste of completion wafting on my tongue like the icy fall of artificial snow. All dramatics aside, it was a tough session at Mountain High, and I got a little cranky when I couldn't land the tricks I knew I was capable of. Call it exhaustion or maybe just not wanting to injure myself with a baby on the way, but I am a little ashamed to say I bowed out on the biggest jump of the night. Thankfully my Midwestern buddy Taylor hit it hard and showed his typical prowess on a board, but as for me, the last leg was certainly the toughest. However, after a solid four hours of riding the snow, I had done it – the Day of Boardacalypse had come to a close, and I survived.

There's a video on my website if you really want to experience the Trishredathon for all its worth, although I'm going to tell you this is certainly something you need to do yourself if you can manage. I owe a big thanks to Russell, Mitchel, Justin, Tim S., Taylor, Tim J. and Tyler for joining me along the way, and Korey for planning. A special double-thanks to Mitchel for completing two out of the three sports (three out of four, if you include skimboarding). I hear he has been training on the skateboard, and so next time I am confident we will stand side-by-side as finishers in one of the greatest challenges Southern California board-riders can undertake. We were blessed to live there and blessed to shred the gnar.

Triple thanks goes out to my wife Katie for supporting this absurd dream, as well as shooting video of me at the skatepark (she was the only pregnant lady there, that I can guarantee!), as well as my daughter Ellie for being born and unknowingly becoming the catalyst for one of the greatest board-riding adventures of my life. I can't wait to take you with me!

Here is a little more on the SoCal locales mentioned in this piece:

Mt. Baldy is Los Angeles' closest ski and snowboard destination, which it boasts heartily. On a clear day, you can even see the ocean from the summit! Being so close to a rather warm city, this mountain rarely has good snow. However, during my first ski season in Los Angeles we got dumped on and I had my first true powder day there. That year they were also selling digital season passes for $100, so needless to say it was an amazing winter. It is a small mountain with some rideable terrain, tree skiing, and a couple icy slopes. Overall, it is fun and kind of a "locals" mountain. They have events all year long, including lots of music festivals and brewery competitions.

www.mtbaldyskilifts.com

Hammerland is one of LA's best surf spots. I have mentioned it before, but here is a little breakdown on how to access it. To get here is a walk no matter what. You can park at the busy El Porto parking lot and, if El Porto isn't satisfying your eyes for a surf, walk (or skate) about a quarter-mile north to see if the waves peeling off the jetty are any good. This was the spot where Russell taught me about paddling out adjacent to jetties and the sort-of "conveyor-belt" effect. El Porto/Hammerland can have a pretty long paddle out, so this tip became key. It seems to apply to all jetties in my experience, but keep far enough away from the rocks or all is lost!

The other option is to park on the north side of the mega ugly factory/smokestacks that mark El Porto, where Grand Avenue turns into El Segundo Beach. I am sure with a little Google search, I could figure out what these abominations are to give you a more accurate description, but I won't give them the honor. On the north side there is a parking lot that in the morning is only $4, but goes up to $9 after ten. So get there early and, when you leave, give your ticket to the next guy to stick it to The Man! It is a shorter walk from here, and a little more pleasant. Don't be deceived on your walk though – the waves you see *before* you approach the jetty may look rideable, but they really aren't. Believe me, I've tried. Multiple times.

Both sides of the jetty can break at the same time, so stand on top, pick your side and paddle out! Or paddle around…if you dare! I will say the north side tends to be hollower and more closed out, while the south side has longer rides, though I've caught plenty of waves on both.

Culver City Skatepark was my first real "local" park, and re-mained my favorite for the duration of my time in LA. I spent many afternoons here, and even once rode my bike the 4.7 miles to get there (the return was brutal). It is truly a masterpiece of a skatepark, with a bowl that deserves awards and a street course to match. "Old" gnarlers come on Saturday mornings and bring boomboxes to shred to the sounds of 80s punk – and they really do shred! Airs abound while egos take a seat. Watching these guys is a treat and they are not too proud to teach you a thing or two about bowl riding if you are bold enough to ask.

After a couple years of skating this park though, and meeting great friends along the way (Josh Andrew the hippie actor, being one of them), scooters became popular and quickly took over like a bad fungus. Not that I have anything against them really (I kind of do), but it is just a more accessible sport, and so *every kid in the city* seems to ride one. Whatever...just skate before school gets out and you'll be fine. And say hi to Eric while you're there, who keeps watch over this place like a father hawk over his nest.

Mtn High is the *next* closest mountain to Los Angeles (followed by Snow Valley and then Big Bear/Snow Summit, if you're counting). My first time here was with my buddy Eric when I was in LA for my last semester of film school. We caught a great snow day and hit some jumps that were way beyond our skill level. Our sixteen-year-old skater-selves took over as we beat ourselves up and did so with a smile. After my return to LA, I never made it to Mtn High with quite the same gusto. A big chunk of the mountain was often closed, though I did catch a nice session on my birthday one time where some guys offered me a mysterious looking drink on the chair lift (both Mtn High and Big Bear offer free riding on your birthday, by the way). A few years later we discovered that they have a super cheap deal on night riding from 5:00PM-10:00PM. With four guys, it could get as low as $20/ticket, which led to several Sunday night sessions after church. Drive home and sleep in the back seat before your return to work Monday morning – another perk to living in Southern California!

www.mtnhigh.com

THE SEARCH FOR A SECRET SPOT

THE SPRING OF 2014 was a tumultuous one. My wife and I had just had our first child, moved, and started a new job all in a week's worth of time. Naturally (and like a terrible dad), I kept trying to surf as much as possible, despite my new responsibilities. And naturally, like an amazing wife, Katie encouraged it! What a lucky guy I am...

Los Angeles is a big city – everyone knows that. So of course, in an overpopulated city, the beaches are just as overpopulated, if not more so, thanks to tourism. It is not uncommon to surf El Porto with just about a yard of space between you and the surfers on either side of you. Look down the beach for a better spot and you won't find one – surfers upon surfers upon surfers for as far as the waves are breaking. It reminded me of ants crawling over each other to climb the hill with a kernel of corn to impress the Queen. Manage to catch a wave and you're dodging the more leisurely beach goers and unsupervised children, all of which don't seem to understand basic laws of motion (Surfer + Heavy surfboard + Force in motion = Hospital Visit). And so, after too many sessions surfing mediocre beach breaks with the rest of the city, Russell and I decided it was time to find our secret spot.

Ever-hopeful people, we knew that with the 75 miles of coastline that LA County has to offer, surely we would be able to find *something* no one else was surfing. It might have been a little smaller, maybe more crumbly, but the crowds were killing us. Of course, I had my spot in Dockweiler, but summers are not great for this beach break, and Russell wasn't on board for surfing here yet. I write "yet" because he would later acknowledge Dockweiler as a decent surf spot (victory!).

I was living in Redondo Beach at the time, and this was the nearest unexplored territory for us both. On a particularly cold spring morning, we had checked out the Redondo Beach jetty and watched a surfer duck-dive about twelve times to get to a choppy, wind-blown wave. We talked ourselves out of attempting this one and nearly headed back home for a dip in the hot tub. However, our inner surf spirit told us to keep driving south, towards Palos Verdes, which was entirely unsearched territory for us both.

Palos Verdes, or PV, is basically paradise in my book. Tucked far away from freeways, it is on the far south end of Los Angeles, which is probably why it took me years to find out it even existed. Unlike most of Los Angeles, PV houses are huge with massive yards, and most of them are nestled upon a cliff overlooking the Pacific with a view of the Channel Islands on a clear day. It is really the closest thing to Hawai'i in Southern California (as far as I can tell). With wide-eyed wonderment, we wandered through its streets, trying to find a beach. With a right turn past a beautiful church, down a road through the main PV plaza and another right towards the coast, we found the parking lot for a school. It must have been spring break or something, because no one was there. We passed by a gazebo that rather romantically looked out to the north with a clear view of the entire Los Angeles coast – another reason to love this town.

I wrote that it was choppy in Redondo, but the wide peninsula of Palos Verdes managed to block some of that on this particular day, which is why when we looked down off of the gazebo we found some pretty rideable waves. We watched a couple surfers catch something, confirming our suspicions, and then decided to suit up and head down the cliff.

Cliff sounds a lot more dangerous than it really was…a paved path that led from the parking lot, past a country club, and down to a little cove is more accurate (but less epic). We traversed some rocks – no problem with our booties on – and hopped into the water. The other surfers had mysteriously disappeared, leaving this new and unknown spot to us. It is a little creepy surfing a seemingly half decent spot alone for the first time. You can't help but wonder if all the other surfers in the city know something you don't know that's keeping them away; meanwhile, you paddle around in shark-infested waters, a sewage dump, or poisonous urchin-covered rocks hidden just inches below the water. On this day, though, it wasn't long before we managed to catch a few waves, marking it as a good session.

After we got home I did a little research and found out the spot was far from secret, even having its own Surfline page. PV Cove is what they call it, and though we experienced none of it that day, I discovered the entire area was littered with localism. Maybe it was a secret spot after all, and somebody wanted to keep it that way…

We would return several months later to surf the Cove, this time noticing a peak that was white-capping a quarter-mile south of us. We paddled all the way there to find a little lineup on a nice left-hander. Knowing PV's reputation at this point, I advised Russell to wait his turn in the lineup (he has a tendency of paddling to the top, making friends, and then surfing wherever he wants; which

127

works, by the way). We did, but when my turn came, a local who had just shredded, and I mean *shredded*, paddled right in front of me and caught the next one. The pattern continued as about three surfers, two of whom were old enough to know better, dominated the spot for the ten-to-fifteen of us who were out there. I got pretty peeved at PV that day, not being one to tolerate localism. Some say it is just part of the sport, but I never understood the ownership one feels over a spot of ocean that we all share. I am happy to say that Los Angeles is widely a friendly place out on the water, but PV is like taking a step back a few decades, where you might get your leash snapped or tires slashed just for paddling out.

But I digress...the search for a secret spot.

So, PV Cove was okay, but not exactly what we were looking for. We decided to take our search north, hoping for a little seldom-surfed corner of Malibu to call our own. And then, one day while I was entering data at my very unsurfery desk job, Russell sends me this:

Whaaaaaatt?!?!? (Photo by Jinhee Joung)

My jaw dropped. Where was this wave? How did he find it? I later learned that Russell had happened across a beautiful spot that was weirdly untouched by most surfers. It was really rocky, and near some other incredible spots, which perhaps diverted most riders away from this hidden gem. It was also relatively dog-friendly, which was a plus for Misteak, Russell's happy mutt.

So where is this amazing spot? I'm not telling you.

C'mon, don't get mad. Can you blame me? I mean, this wave is great – short paddle out, reef break with long rights and the occasional lefts. It's not perfect – you have to literally dodge rocks on your ride in – but I've seen it get rather big here with small crowds. Sorry. Maybe if we surf together in LA I'll take you there.

I am remiss to report to you, however, that since discovering this spot, it has indeed become more populated. Great minds think alike, and so many a surfer must have been on the same quest as we were. Still, for a full summer we surfed this break as much as we could, and I will hold that summer dear in my mind forever.

And so I use the last little space on this page to charge you to find your own secret spot, wherever you are. It may be the same one we did or on the opposite coast. It may take only two attempts or it may take twenty years. But either way, when you find what you're looking for, you'll be glad you searched down new and untrodden roads, because sometimes, new roads are the ones that may just lead you home.

Okay, want another hint to where this spot may or may not be? Take a listen to this song and read the lyrics. It was written about the gem, and may be of a little assistance:

STANDOUT

There's a standout headed for me
I see it coming up through the seaweed
Well God bless the ocean and God bless the sea
And when this wave comes He'll be blessing me

There's a swell moving through this week
And if we skip work, we'll hit the peak
Oh I know it's early, but you can sleep
After you've caught twenty waves at least

There's a spot outside of town
Where the rocks'll make you run aground
But the waves are better, so just surf around
Until you hit one, then we're hospital-bound

There's a standout headed for us
We can both get on it I trust
When an A-frame comes, ride them we all we must
It's a party wave, surf or bust

I'm always happy to be out on the waves
Following that narrow way
If it's peaceful out there, it's probably flat today
But we're surfing and so we're okay

When you want to find peace, go and ride those waves
Somehow surfing makes it all okay

A FATHER'S FIRST "DAY"

FATHER'S DAY IS WHEN Dad gets special treatment, right? You go to church and then out to eat where he wants, buy him something cool (not a tie), and mow the lawn so he doesn't have to. And so, when my first Father's Day came, I went into it with that mindset – my day. And sure enough, when my day came I heard over and over, "It's your day! Do what you want!"

But what did I want? If I *really* had what I wanted, I would have gone on a surf adventure that lasted all day, to a break my family probably would not have enjoyed, and eaten tacos afterwards at T2 Tacos, a mediocre taco place that would years later disappear for reasons unknown to this author. And that's not because I didn't *want* to hang out with my family – I love my family – but if you give me a day and call it mine, I'm going to do something I love doing, but probably don't get to do that often; which in this case was go on a surf adventure to the secret spot in the aforementioned chapter.

But what kind of a Father's Day is that? Dad out in the ocean with some friends while the family hangs back home? It might as well be called Bachelor's Day. A father isn't a father, after all, without his family. So maybe Father's Day is less about doing what I want to do, and more about being a good dad? There was just one problem – I still kept hearing "It's your day" and I really wanted to go surfing. Therein lay my issue, but also my point: life is about balance.

When I graduated high school I asked my dad to give me one piece of advice for the future, one thing to guide me as I embarked on my first solo journey as a sort-of adult. He said the best advice he could give was to keep life in balance the best you can – work, school, family, God, hobbies – all in balance with each other. It has been many years since I received that advice, and regrettably I still haven't figured out how to do it well, though I am a lot closer now than I was back then.

I ended up spending my Father's Day at church, and then going to lunch somewhere I enjoyed, but wouldn't have been my first choice (I didn't want to subject my family to cheap tacos, particularly my mother-in-law, who was in town at the time). After that, I spent a good bit of time with my family and then went for a quick surf at a nearby break I have been meaning to try, followed by a movie at a friend's house. It felt like a pretty balanced day, and so it was good.

So, my first Father's Day was a mix of selfishness and sacrifice. I am not sure if I did it right, but it at least felt like one more step towards a life of balance, and that is a success to me.

SUPERMOON SURFING

YOU'VE SEEN THAT NIGHT surfing scene in *Point Break*, right? The one where he catches a huge wave and then hooks up with the girl right there on the beach. It's totally fake, day-for-night shooting. Or is it? (It is.) But night surfing isn't! And California is one of the best places to accomplish this dream-like feat, while also fulfilling your ideal of becoming a little more like Johnny Utah.

It was a brisk September evening in 2015 when the famed Supermoon was set to grace our hemisphere. In case you don't know (because I didn't), a Supermoon is when the moon is the closest it gets to the earth, and on this evening it was rising at about 8:00PM, which was just about perfect for a night surf session. We chose Leo Carrillo, because typically you can surf here at night anyway since the road and its collection of streetlights and car headlights kind-of-sort-of illuminate your way. The wave is fairly predictable, breaking only in one spot, furthering the reason to make this your night surf haven.

Up until this point, I had never tried night surfing. For some reason, surfing in the dark and sharks seem to go hand in hand in the minds of most common folk, and I was no different. But Russell had done it several times before at this very spot, so I trusted my good friend with my life.

A rule of thumb for night surfing is to head out a little before the sky is totally dark, just so you can get a feel for how the waves are breaking that night. Dusk is, however, when sharks feed, so stay smart. My wife got me one of those Shark Banz anklets (they also make a leash that Russell's girlfriend got *him*) that is supposed to keep away *most* sharks. However, it is said to not work on Great Whites, which are most common in LA, so buyer beware! The good thing about surfing North Malibu is that it breaks fairly shallow, so in my mind that means no *big* sharks can swallow you up. This is probably totally untrue, but at least it sets my mind at rest.

So, we paddled out a little after the sun disappeared, with just enough light to see what we were doing. The break was crowded that night, which lets you know we weren't the most original thinkers in LA County to consider Supermoon surfing potentially epic and unforgettable. The swell was quite good too, producing four-to-six-foot sets at the mellow reef break. On the bigger sets, it was actually a little scary because you would just bob up and down, hearing and feeling like something big was coming, but you couldn't see a wave until it was about ten yards away. A quick turn and a mad paddle, or an even madder paddle and a quick duck dive were your options. We were just hoping it wasn't a standout (frequent at this break), because that could mean taking one on the head on, or near, a large set of rocks that mark the inside section of the wave. A little danger never did anyone too much harm though, did it? Johnny Utah survived (but Bodhi was another story…)

Such was the first hour or so until it happened – the Supermoon rose. It was a surreal experience, floating in the water next to Mitchel and Rochelle as the large red moon slowly lifted above the Santa Monica city lights. It was massive like a painting, as if Van Gogh had set up his easel on that very rock and was painting a new *Starry Night* in between sets. Really, it was like nothing I had ever seen. The moon has always intrigued me, often causing me to stop and gaze at the giant rock while it cast a pale blue splendor over any and everything in sight. That night it was certainly no different, and only more magical with the lure of long right-handers gracing what had become an unforgettable evening.

Have you ever wondered what happens to all the waves that go unsurfed every night? Millions of beautiful rides are missed in the darkness all across the planet. It's a shame really. But there is also something kind of sovereign about it, reminding us that every ride is a gift, and if the God of the oceans wishes to waste beautiful A-frames every evening, then that is up to Him. You have no choice but to accept it.

But in some places, and at some instances, those waves don't have to go unridden. If you haven't gone for a night surf yet, I hope the above story inspires you! And if you should choose to take the plunge, here are a few more tips to make your night magical.

- **Schedule your surf on a full moon:** That giant luminescent ball in the sky makes a huge difference in your session. (Who would have thought?)
- **Always night surf with friends:** It is a bit dangerous out there because you often can't see the waves or other surfers until they are a few yards away. You need guys around you to

keep an eye out in case something should happen, and vice versa. But how do you see your friends in the dark?

- **Bring glow sticks**: I realized this on my second night surf paddle out when a few guys had glow sticks, but my crew did not. When one of them dropped in, it was easy to see. When I dropped in – not so much. There were a couple of near-collisions that could have been easily preventable with a little illumination. If you want to take it even farther, try buying some neon wires and strapping them to your boards and wetsuits for a very *Tron*-esque surf session.

- **Get to the break before the sun sets**: Even at a familiar break, it is always good to take a look at the ocean in full light in case the particular swell is bringing something unexpected. Also, check ahead for tides and swell direction so you are well-informed. I know that is normal surf routine, but the stakes are higher for a night surf if you're not prepared for the conditions.

Johnny Utah makes it look easy, but night surfing is dangerous! Always do your best to stay safe, safe, safe!

I mentioned that the moon has always had a magic allure for me. One night, not while surfing but after working, a particularly beautiful moon was out and so I wrote this song during my drive home.

LUNA

I've always been
Drawn to your beauty
Lured to a far-off place
And I don't think it's a
Man on the moon
'Cause I see a
Woman's face

Round like a pearl
Bright like the light
That shines from a
Lover's smile
Whenever you cast
Your glow down on me
I'm bound to stare
For awhile

Ah Luna, I know
That you simply must be
Created by One
Much greater than you or me

You cast a blue
Over the world
O'er all that I
Can see

I know it's a hue
Hemmed in wonder
Disguised as
Melancholy

Luna you're like
A magnet of light
I can't help but
Stare until
All that's around you
Blurs out of view
A black wall and
Window sill

And should you wane
Should you disappear
I'd throw a lasso
To bring you back here
Yes, I would fight the blackest
        night…
Tell the stars to dim their lights…
Run this whole world ragged
        right…
Just for you…
Luna, my dear

LOVE AND SURFING

I HAD JUST HAD an awesome surf session at Redondo Beach – pretty big waves, a couple great left-handers with probably the best snaps I've ever done. As I showered off afterwards, it struck me just how good I felt, and I was reminded of how much I love surfing.

You might be saying, "Of course you love surfing, Rick, you're writing a book about it." You're right. But sometimes you forget what you love, don't you? For instance, you love your spouse, right? But how often do you take them out on a date or shower them with compliments, just because it's true? You love your kids, but how much time did you spend on your phone the last time you took them to the park? Not to sound judgmental, but often times our actions don't back up our decisions.

And sometimes it is just because we simply need a reminder.

As I reflected, I remembered all of the reasons I *almost* didn't surf: it was chilly outside today and I didn't really feel like surfing – call me a fair-weather surfer, but sometimes you can't help it. To make matters worse, I couldn't find any friends to come with and I have a hurt rib from a softball run-in in the outfield. (Keep your head up out there!) There were plenty of reasons not to paddle out, but afterwards, I am sure glad I did! Life is the same way – I don't always *feel* like loving my wife or my kids. I sometimes don't feel like doing a good job at work or praying or eating kale. In these situations we must make a choice and then back it up with action. And what is the result? Usually, the wayward feelings come back and you are in love again. With your wife, your kids, God, and even sometimes surfing.

A little more on Redondo Beach: It is featured in the classic surf film *The Endless Summer*, but the break in that movie is far from what you will typically find there today. I'm talking about a ten-foot difference in wave height. The sand bar shifted since that epic film was shot – as they often do – and now you're lucky to get a head-high day here, which is what I had the day I wrote this piece.

There is a groin that splits Redondo, creating North and South sections that differ slightly. The north is typically smaller and breaks closer to the beach. The south side will break farther out and just a little more – how should I put it? – wild. Something about that wave is unpredictable, like riding a horse that isn't broken yet, which is fun in a way, but scary on those rare big days. There is a little sand bar somewhere that churns up a really enticing section, but for some reason it is incredibly difficult to catch; and also incredibly easy to get sucked into. I am still not sure what it is, but I would venture to say that there is something sinister going on there under the sea…

I actually went to surf Redondo one day with Tyler and there were cops everywhere – someone had spotted a dead body and the

Coast Guard was trying to find it. Mark that as the only surf session I have ever had where after every wave I skittled my feet on the sand below expecting to hit a lifeless hand.

Anyway, the best place to park for Redondo is on Esplanade just after Veterans park. Free street parking abounds, unless it is a beautiful Saturday, in which case you might have to head in a block or two and walk to the long stairs that take you down to the shore. There are also some quality skate spots just along the beach side-walk (including a new skatepark built right on the pier!), as well as a handful of volleyball courts. Keep heading south and you will hit RAT Beach. It all kind of runs together, if you ask me, though RAT seems slightly less surfable as it usually breaks really shallow. I have seen pictures of choice waves there though; so don't discount it if you are thinking of paddling out in the South Bay.

And finally, there is a section north of the pier, and also north of the marina called Redondo Beach Breakwater. I always thought this was part of Hermosa Beach, but I learned later that it is indeed Redondo. The parking here once was glorious (since this book is all about nostalgia, I'll indulge myself…): There was a lot right on the water that was seldom full and you only paid $1/hour in a little box where you folded the dollar and put it in on your space slot. If you were waiting for the last wave and ten minutes *after* you initially started your hour, odds were that the security guard who lazily drove around collecting money wouldn't be there.

As for the break, it was typically small, but for someone reason always fun. I've had beautiful sunset rides here on tiny little waves. But with the right swell, it gets big and hollow. Guys line up to get barreled with cameras on the shore capturing the better surfers' rides. I remember one such session where Mitchel, Aaron, and I felt quite out of our league paddling out at the main break, and so we walked down looking for something rideable. All we found were folding walls of water, but we paddled out anyway. Afterwards, there was a kid with a board snapped in half in the parking lot, looking pretty pissed that his epic surf session was interrupted. Amazed, I asked a couple questions, but he wasn't in the mood to talk. (Come on, Rick, read the room...er, parking lot.)

Just to burst your bubble, the parking is handled by one of those fancy apps now, and the price fluctuates based on demand. I've seen it as high as $6/hour, though it teeters in the $2-3 range on most weekdays. Ah well, nothing gold can stay, as they say.

It's still a nice place to surf.

FOLLOW ME

Follow my example, as I follow the example of Christ. (1 Corinthians 11:1)

I'VE FOUND THAT WHEN you want to do something, it's best with other people, but also best not to *wait around* for those people. This applies heavily to skating and surfing, particularly in your thirties. But I am notoriously bad about planning little surf excursions and then inviting everyone I know and their dogs to join. (Let's say that means literal and figurative dogs; as in, "what up dog?!") What ends up happening is much stress over organizing times, places, carpools, and board-borrowing, and little time actually enjoying the surfing. Sometimes a simple trip with a couple of friends is all you need for a good time, and honestly, my best sessions are like that.

Still, a fun day at the Dockweiler fire pits with all your closest mates is always a tempting offer.

However, sometimes you invite all your friends and no one wants to join, or everyone is too busy, or it's cold and the waves are bad. In these cases, it's easy to call it a day and play *Skate* on your PlayStation instead. But too much of that, and you've lost all your surf-muscles, you're fifteen pounds heavier, and you've watched the entire series of *Home Improvement*...twice. No good. There are times you just have to pave your own path, surf alone, and enjoy it for what it is. Who knows, maybe you'll meet a new friend out on the water that also enjoys tiny surf and cold mornings. Or maybe you'll just see a whale.

I am sweating as I write this because I just went skateboarding at 9:00PM by myself at the old middle school where I grew up skating. Had I waited for a like-minded friend to join, I would have likely fallen asleep early after a particularly busy day of work, the carbohydrates from my dinner and dessert freely bloating inside. Instead, I went out and started working on a new trick! I don't think thirty qualifies as an "old dog" in the real world, but in skateboarding, I'm semi-retired; and this "old dog" is still learning new tricks. So, follow me if you can, and let's shred into the night!

This same principle applies to our faith. There is no need to wait for someone else to "help me" get spiritual or bring me closer to God. I can do that right now with the help of the Holy Spirit. Now don't get me wrong – I believe firmly in our need to grow in our faith as a community and in no way endorse "Lone Wolf Christianity." That verse in 1 Corinthians above requires a leader and a follower; I am just saying that sometimes *you* might be the leader.

LET GO

A FEW WEEKS AFTER my second daughter was born, all I wanted
to do was surf. It had been a while, but a friend invited me out and
so the prospect was there. A couple contingencies blocked my path
though: my oldest daughter needed to be napping and my newborn
needed to stay quiet *while* the oldest was napping...all successfully
in our tiny two-bedroom apartment. As my wife and I rocked our
baby to sleep, watching another episode of *Fixer Upper*, I kept a keen
eye on the clock, knowing my friend was paddling out at 4:00PM
and that it was already past 3:00. Unfortunately, the television could
not drown out the sound of *both* my daughters crying as the sweet
possibility of surf was slipping away before my reddening eyes.

I tried hard to not let my hopes get up for a surf session. When
that was becoming less possible, I tried hard to let go of even those
hopes. Unfortunately, I found myself doing anything but. Down-
right anxious, all I wanted was for the kids to be quiet so I had a
good excuse to go surfing. It was consuming me, making me angry,
irritable, no fun to be around. My desire to surf had won out against

logic, emotion, and even love.

Eventually things quieted down and I did get to go surfing, but as I drove to the beach, I couldn't help but feel ashamed of my behavior and attitude, and so I decided something had to change. All of the irritation going along with a simple desire actually *decreased* the overall enjoyment of the thing I wanted.

Being a father means abandoning the self for the sake of others, but our natural tendency is to hold on to whatever we can. The more kids you have, the less self you have to hold on to. Losing control of the time you once enjoyed and took for granted, you're practically forced into self*less*ness. But what happens when our body kicks back and we fight for those neglected desires? Are we supposed to just *make* ourselves less selfish? I think that's where some divine inspiration helps:

> *Do nothing out of selfish ambition or vain conceit. Rather, in humility value others above yourselves, not looking to your own interests but each of you to the interests of the others. (Philippians 2:3-4 ESV)*

> *For this very reason, make every effort to supplement your faith with virtue, and virtue with knowledge, and knowledge with self-control, and self-control with steadfastness, and steadfastness with godliness, and godliness with brotherly affection, and brotherly affection with love. (2 Peter 1:5-7 ESV)*

Start with faith...a saving faith in Christ and faith that God is working on us through His Spirit. That leads to virtues such as patience, love, and goodness. Add to that knowledge: knowing the scriptures and what God wants to make us into, as well as His power to do so. All of that together leads to self-control when we get into these situations and, as those situations become increasingly difficult, suffering kicks in. Ultimately, we become more like Christ, which finds its culmination in loving others.

It is a long road, but at least we are given clear steps to take. Always remember though, this doesn't start with our own ability, but rather faith.

> *For it is by grace you have been saved, through faith—and this is not from yourselves, it is the gift of God—not by works, so that no one can boast. For we are God's handiwork, created in Christ Jesus to do good works, which God prepared in advance for us to do. (Ephesians 2:8-10 ESV)*

Letting go is one of the most difficult things to do in life, and a journey God has had me on for several years. I wrote this song in response to a word from God that I heard while driving down the 405 freeway one evening. It's a conversation with God, an honest back and forth, as well as a story about the progression of letting go. Also, I'd say it applies to surfing as well as to life.

LET GO (ABANDON)

"Oh, I'm not asking you
To abandon who
You are or who you wanted to be
I was just hoping you'd
Let go of these things that get
In between the love of
You and me"

You asked for my life
And I gave it away
Only to take it all right back
(to) control my destiny

You said that I died
Right along with You
Then how come there's
Still these stubborn dreams
That I'm holding onto?

"Let go, let go" is what You said
But letting go is what I dread
Oh, I don't know how to let go
So I'm holding on instead
You asked for my life
But I held it back
To do all the things I wanted to

That I claimed that you asked
Then one day You called
On me to let it go
But I said, "That's who I am and
What I do, so no."

"Oh, I'm not asking you
To abandon who you are
Or who you wanted to be
I'm trying to remove
All that's gotten through
That keeps you from
Trusting me"

You said that I died
But then you raised me to life
A truer version of myself
Than I could have designed
So why not let go
Abandon it all?
Because when God tells you to let go
Man, listen to that call

"Let go, let go" is what You said
But letting go is what I dread
Oh, I don't know how to let go

So I'll trust in You instead
"Oh, I'm not asking you
To exchange all who
You are or who you
Wanted to be
I'll just say with love
That I am enough
You will find what you seek
In Me"

PART FIVE
LETTING GO

THE CURRENT STATE OF SURFING

IT WAS THE KIND of night that Southern California dreams are made of. Some friends of mine had miraculously secured a campsite at Leo Carrillo the same weekend a modest swell was set to come through. On top of that, it was a full moon, so we would be able to paddle out at 10:00PM, just as the street parking closed and all the day-trippers would have to make the hour-long trip back to LA wishing they could have stayed longer. Yes, all was set for the perfect end to summer...that is, until about thirty other surfers had the same genius idea we did.

"Since when did night surfing become *day* surfing?!" one guy lamented out loud, verbalizing the obvious disappointment we all felt. To make matters worse, about a third of the people on the water were some of the most obnoxious surfers I have ever encountered. I had one guy literally run into me as I was dropping in, and then on the next wave *drop in* right in front of me – two huge surfing faux pas, back-to-back. When I called him out on it, claiming the inside position, his response was an uncaring (or possibly oblivious),

"Dude…"

Despite the circumstances, I managed to catch a handful of nice waves, though my friends were not so lucky. The next day, however, this time with the sun shining on a rare warm-enough-to-surf-without-a-wetsuit day, it was more of the same. Less obnoxious (thank the Lord), but as I paddled to wait my turn in the lineup, I noticed that the same five people were catching every wave. I quickly learned that there was no such thing as a lineup at this spot, and if you wanted to surf, you had to head to the deep inside zone to force a supposed right of way; and this only worked if no one else decided to drop in in front of you, or if you could swing in under them before they got too far. It was chaos, a zoo, one of the least respectful surf environments I have ever been in, and ultimately, no fun.

Maybe I am being a little over-dramatic (I *did* manage to catch some great waves), but at the end of the day I couldn't help but feel disheartened. I always thought there were rules to surfing, etiquette and respect to keep peace on the water as we try to all enjoy the same aquatic space. Courtesies such as "the inside man gets the wave" and "taking turns through the lineup" have governed my surfing for years. But if you check out any Malibu surf camera on any given day, I guarantee you will see one surfer drop in on another in the first set that rolls through. It seems the culture of many Southern California spots has become "Do what it takes to surf a wave, regardless of who is on it already, if you have the right of way, or whether or not you're being a dick."

It's not like that everywhere. And maybe that's just the way surfing has to be (after all, many of the best spots in the world have the worst localization). But competing for a little piece of water that isn't even yours to begin with just seems to me the very opposite of the surfing spirit – the camaraderie, the peace, the pursuit. Call me an idealist, but I think surfers can be better to each other out on the water, even at a crowded spot, just as we can be good towards each other as we coexist on land and in life.

Vying for the same goal of scoring an excellent wave does not have to mean drowning the guy next to you just to do it, which is what it may turn to if we don't realize that the waves we are riding have nothing to do with us outside of our shared desire for them. We had no part in creating them; no say in shaping the ocean floor that caused them, and in no way can claim them as our own. So why do we act that way as we ride them?

I say, with respect to each other, the ocean and our shared love of surfing, let's take some advice from Bill and Ted and just be excellent to each other. It might just make our surfing lives better, and our beaches a little more enjoyable.

"So in everything, do to others what you would have them do to you, for this sums up the Law and the Prophets." (Matthew 7:12)

"This is what the LORD *says,*
He who appoints the sun
  to shine by day,
who decrees the moon and stars
  to shine by night,
who stirs up the sea
  so that its waves roar—
  the LORD *Almighty is His name:" (Jeremiah 31:35)*

...LOST BOARD

I HAD BEEN RIDING the Al Merrick that Ty gave me for years and was really getting used to the board. It was skinny, long, and thick in the middle. Easy to duck dive and held an edge for the drop on big days, but not too thin or short on smaller days. I was riding it the first day I remember someone giving me a compliment on my surfing after a little drop and quick little off-the-lip thing (it was hardly a maneuver, but always feels good when someone notices). But as they say, all good things must come to an end, and the end of the Al Merrick was hardly worthy of its epic life.

Every surfer has a roof rack tradition that he or she follows to secure boards to the roof (can you see where this is heading?), should that be the situation he or she operates under. I developed a nice bungee/rope double-tie combo on my 1997 Honda Civic Hatchback, using the aftermarket roof racks from my 2005 Kia Rio Cinco (RIP) that I screwed onto the Honda. This setup carried on to the 2006 Toyota Prius (also RIP) with the Inno roof racks that I bought my wife as a birthday present, thinking that she genuinely wanted them. (I later found out she only wanted racks because I was ruining the interior of her car by lying wet, sticky surfboards in between the seats.) But after years of double strapping my boards, I decided that maybe I was wasting time tying when I could spend that extra thirty-to-sixty seconds surfing. Simultaneously, for some reason I thought it would be a good idea to work out a new bungee technique that would also be faster.

I am a big proponent of creative problem solving, but all of those turned out to be bad ideas.

Katie and I were heading to El Porto on a sunny Sunday afternoon. We were almost free of the onramp from the 405 to the 105 when we heard a loud bang. I looked to the rear view mirror in horror to find my beloved Al Merrick detached from our car. Not only did it fly *off* of our roof, but it also almost hit a car, was sent airborne and proceeded to fall about 150 feet below off of the elevated freeway and into a fenced-off parking lot.

We need to save my board! I thought as I instructed my wife on how to exit the freeway and backtrack to where it looked like the board landed. A few wrong turns later, I found it in the middle of a Metro employee parking lot that I had to hop a high fence to get into. The board fared well, all things considered: all of the fins were still in, but the tail was smashed. A couple of punctures on the bottom of the board and slightly crunched-in rails rounded off the damage that should have been far greater. The problem was (one of many) that I was on my way to surf with Russell, and even my valiant Al Merrick was unrideable, lest I wanted a severely water-logged board.

But lo! Hope arose like the crest of El Porto's sun-glistened break. Russell's brother was moving north and wanted to sell his ... *Lost* Mayhem fish shape. I had ridden the board once and it wasn't bad, so I thought I would give it a shot and see if it was worth the purchase. The board was basically new, a 6'8" fish with a quad-fin setup that could be switched to a thruster (or penta-fin, should excessive fin usage be desired). I rode it for about a month before deciding that this was the board for me, encouraged by a seemingly random video gig that appeared that earned me more than enough to make the purchase.

The wind in your hair will make you feel anything but...Lost.
(Photo by Sean Powers)

The Mayhem took a little while to get used to. It is wide, with a unique concave bottom that causes the rails to really dig in if you cut too hard. It is thin up top but very thick in the middle, helping you get into smallish waves with proper weight distribution. I ended up preferring the thruster setup, finding that it gave me more control on turns without sacrificing too much fish-like maneuverability. I remember wondering if I had made a mistake the first few months

I had the board, struggling to get into waves and finding the drag from digging-in inhibiting. However, on a consistently three-foot day at El Porto, while surfing with Russell and Dan (another surfing friend of ours from Russell's climbing gym), I felt for the first time that this board really shone.

The Mayhem caught tiny waves when Russell and Dan could not (they had recently purchased pretty short boards from a local shop that required just a bit more water underneath them), which always makes you feel like you're a rock star, particularly when your wave count starts to exceed your friends' by several. I told Russell that this was the first day I really felt comfortable on the Mayhem, to which he replied, "That makes me feel sad." It had been months and he always feels kind of guilty whenever money and surfing mix (he rarely accepts gas money, if ever); I suppose he felt a little responsible for my lack those prior months.

"It's alright," I replied, "this board is fine." It was fine and still is. It takes a while to get used to a new board and I am not very good at surfing anyway, so why should I be any different? The tragedy of my Al Merrick turned into what is likely a more fitting board for the kind of waves I ride. And so I will say with confidence that everything happens for a reason, even boards flying off of your roof conveniently timed with board sales and freelance jobs.

"In their hearts humans plan their course, but the LORD establishes their steps." (Proverbs 16:9)

As for the Al Merrick: I got a reasonable verbal quote from Soul Performance, the aforementioned surf shop that also happened to offer me a spot on their skate team after watching my *Skater Dad: the Movie* video (a dream come true, really). It sat in my garage for about a year while I waited for a budget surplus until, when we had decided to move back east, I took it in. "It would cost more than this board is worth to fix it," Mark said, "So unless you have some sentimental attachment…" And he trailed off, not wanting to mention the obvious fate of a green-dumpster tomb. He ended up offering to trade me a skate deck for the board so he could fix it to sell, which I was moderately happy to take. The deck is still sitting in my garage, waiting for its turn as my pool skateboard. I am not sure if it was an even trade, but something for something is better than something turned to nothing.

The lesson here is obvious and two-fold: when you have a good thing going, don't change it up and then try it out with a sixty miles-per-hour test. Maybe ride around the neighborhood a little before heading to the freeway.

Second, look for the good in the bad because it is there. That …*Lost* rests in our bedroom and I sometimes find myself staring at it for long lapses of time. The shape is simply beautiful and invokes the lofty dreams of future cutbacks and buttery smooth snaps. It is also covered in orange wax right now, which is my favorite color. I often imagine myself carving waves on it with long and gentle turns, the ever-increasing speed of a *pump, pump, pump…boost* always the culmination. Of course the mind is more powerful than the body, so whether or not those turns look as good as I see them is up for debate, but a guy can dream, right? I can't say I thought about the Al Merrick like I do this one. I will have to conclude that, like the sport of surfing itself, some things just burrow into your heart when you least expect it, and there find a place to stay.

COLD AT COUNTY LINE

COUNTY LINE IS ONE of those spots that remained largely mystical to me during most of my years in Los Angeles. I had seen glimpses of it, but only over the cliffs of north Malibu/south Ventura. Most of the time we stopped at Leo Carrillo, rarely venturing the 1.2 miles up the road to check out what is likely a better break. I say that because it is far more spread out than Leo Carrillo and its notoriously single catchable location. County Line, on the other hand, feels like a mini-Orange County break in the vein of Trestles or Huntington Beach – really nice waves and a lot of space to catch them – all reef breaks pseudo A-framing off of rocks like a good Malibu wave should.

My first experience here was during a church-wide camping trip a bit *more* up the road at Point Mugu. The waves at Mugu were a gnarly beach break that day – the kind that tear down the sand and cause the beach to slope at a near-45-degree angle. Not good for surfing, but we did enjoy a nice beach baptism a hundred yards down where the waves were less intense. Because the waves were largely unrideable, we decided to pack in a couple of cars and head south on the warmest October day that I can remember. We weren't even wearing wetsuits, which only made it that much better. Anyone who denies global warming just needs to spend a few years in Southern California, where the snow seasons have dropped off dramatically and the summers last that much longer. Of course, as the hipster muse of our time Ben Gibbard said, maybe we're just being rewarded for good behavior with all this equally good weather (a paraphrase).

A large group of us paddled out, many beginners, including Pastor Scott who had just got a Wavestorm. He was excited to ride, as well as Dave and Collie, who were enthusiastic beginners under the wise tutelage of Mitchel and Rochelle. I have to take some time here to mention my wife, who patiently watched our one-year-old on the beach while I went out and had fun. She has done this time after time after time and will never be thanked enough. If we can stop getting pregnant (she's a good-lookin' lady), she will learn to surf one day and I will owe her about a thousand surf sessions. But until then...

I paddled into a rather crowded beach, but again, it was pretty spread out. I have this thing that occurs in my mind when I'm surfing around other people I know that I don't usually surf around (including my wife) – I try really hard to surf well so they will think I am awesome at the sport I love. The problem is, I'm not awesome (competent might be a better term), and when I'm trying hard, I am even worse. All that to say, I don't think I had that many good rides that day. It was fun and a little big, but the crowds and my pride kept me from fully enjoying this amazing spot.

But that should help you realize just how good County Line is – even a bad day can be a good one. I have heard rumors of local-ization, but all I remember is meeting a guy who managed a couple of has-been bands that were trying to stay afloat (pun intended), and this one dude who had the most beautiful bottom turns I have ever seen in person. Power, grace, and a little inside hand tap on the water will be forever burned in my memory by this majestic stranger.

This talk of a bad surf session leads me to the next County Line experience, again with Mitchel and Rochelle, plus our Costa Rican friend Ricardo, who despite growing up near world-class beaches that we Americans will pay thousands of dollars to surf, was a humble beginner. It was the opposite of that warm October day, a true California cold day (which, let's be honest, isn't that cold, relatively speaking). And so, trying hard to be a nice guy, I offered him my good thick wetsuit and I used the borderline spring suit. Bad idea for this Southeastern wimp.

The waves were far from going-off that day. Not even close. The tide was very low, and everyone there (a moderate crowd) was vying for the main break, which was crumbling off of a point at the north end of the beach. I paddled a lot, caught a few, but the lulls in between the sets were brutal, and before long the teeth chattering began. I once read that there are monks that could control their body temperature in the coldest or hottest of situations, just by imagining either an icicle or a fire up their rear ends. I have tried it out on the water, many times...to no avail.

Even after six years of surfing the often-frigid Pacific, my Southern blood still ran thin. I hit a point where the cold outweighed the surf, and so I headed back to the car where I literally ran the heat while I huddled between blankets. Judge me all you want – I know where I come from and I am comfortable with who I am. While the windows fogged, I listened to one of my favorite bands, House of Heroes, play several melodic ballads with ease and energy. Not ideal, but not awful. I fully intended to paddle back out – this was near the end of my time of surfing in Los Angeles, and I knew it could possibly be my last session at County Line for a while. However, my cold bones took far too long to thaw, and by the time I was ready, everyone else had decided to head home.

A truly international crew. And NO ALCOHOL! (Photo by Author)

We hit up the McDonald's on the way home and I thoroughly enjoyed their attempt at a fancy avocado burger, as well as an ice cream. Yes, like a glutton for punishment I began to crave one of their delicious $1 sundaes. Cold as I was, I didn't regret it. That's why cars have heaters! Besides, there's always McDonald's hot $1 coffee!

This piece somehow turned into a story lined with product placement. If you are one of the following people and make some money off of what I wrote, see the contact page on the back and share the love! (Just kidding…but really.)

- The Postal Service song I referenced is called "Sleeping In," off of their album *Give Up*, from Sub Pop records.
- Dave and Colie own a magic card company with Dave's brother Dan. Check them out at www.dananddave.com
- The piece about the monks and their temperature control was read in *Who's Your Caddy* by Rick Reilly, a book given me by Ty Pukatch.
- Do yourself a favor and listen to House of Heroes at www.thehouseofheroes.com, or wherever you stream.
- McDonald's doesn't know I exist and doesn't care about this book, plus the sundaes aren't a dollar anymore...

Speaking of Global Warming, here is another song to warm your heart and expand your mind on the topic. No, it's not political, but it will make you chuckle as well as think a thought or two:

GLOBAL WARMING

Maybe global warming isn't all that
Bad, yeah, I said it
It's hot then cold, the seasons swing
But I haven't seen the city quite this
Green before

I can't remember the last time
It rained like this in Los Angeles
It's clear all year, that's the sunshine
tax
But we pay for it in high rent and
Sitting in traffic all the time

Fear fills us like the food we eat
But my mind chooses a different
reality

Yeah, I know the oceans are rising
I don't deny it
But if I can buy that house a mile in
It'll be beachfront and at least my
Kids can enjoy it (If they're still here)

Fear fills us like the food we eat
But my mind chooses a different
reality
Fear fuels us like gasoline
Light a match and watch the worries
gleam

There's a river that runs through
the city
But "river" is a generous term
Maybe one day it'll be flowing and
churning
As long as the world gets warm

There are worries that flow through
our minds
But there's no need for concern
Because we can all be kind to each
other
As long as our hearts stay warm

Maybe life is all about perspective
Yeah, I mean it
If the world is collapsing all around
I can keep a smile on as I walk
through town
Even if the city is burning down…
Well, no one liked this town anyway
And the sun will still shine on an-
other day
Maybe we will be in a better place
And we can have global warming
to thank

ALMOST SEVEN YEARS

THIS BOOK IS ABOUT my seven years of surfing in Los Angeles, but the truth is, it wasn't quite seven years. *Almost* just made the title too wordy…(that's a joke). I did do a semester of college out in LA and surfed once, which would more accurately fill in the missing months to make it seven years. On that day, though, I paddled out with a bunch of Midwesterners (most of them have been mentioned in this book already), who were used to cold weather, but had never really surfed. I'm not one to talk a big game, but I did admit that I had been surfing about half my life at that point. "Casually surfing" would have been a better way of putting it, because truthfully I hadn't gone out much through middle school or college. (Skateboarding was more my thing.) And so when I paddled out at Venice with these Iowa boys and a hole in my wetsuit, but only lasted about forty-five minutes before going in because I got so cold my vision was going blurry, I lost a lot of street cred. I ended up sitting huddled by the sidewalk wall, trying to stay warm while they surfed for at least another hour. It was miserable, and it took about four years of proving myself as a surfer to regain respect from them (if I even ever did…).

Anyway, the point of all this blunt honesty is that, as I look back at certain milestones in my life, I never quite went the distance. *Almost* seven years in LA. I worked *almost* four years at NBCUniversal (my longest-standing job to-date). The whole reason I moved to Los Angeles was to pursue film and when I made the move, I decided my minimum stay would be ten years. Seven years isn't even an *almost* to ten, so call it what you want, I still fell short.

So what does this mean, hitting "almost" so many times in my life?

Maybe it's a side effect of living on the starting cusp of Millennialism. We are notorious for not committing: to jobs, relationships, cell phone plans, reading books (kudos if you've made it this far). You name it, we've found our way out. I am actually at a point in life where this title of Millennial and all that comes with it really seems to be butting heads with a lot of what I am expected to do as a provider, a father, and even a creative.

Here I am in the South, working six days a week and still not quite making enough to feed my family. Of course, my wife could start working, but who would watch our two daughters? We could hire a daycare or nanny, but we want a parent to be home, plus her salary would probably only just cover the cost of it. And so there goes the savings account, because this world just isn't set up for one-spouse incomes anymore. And surfing? Well, let's just say my once every week or two surf sessions have turned into once every three months. I am skating when I can, but with all this work, who has time? Is this growing up and getting older? Work a lot and then you die? I once read that children smile about ten times more than adults per day, and I think these realities might have something to do with it.

And so here I am, writing this book of reminiscing over the past (almost) seven years that were some of the best years of my life. There was a point during the summer of 2013 where I averaged two-to-four surf sessions a week! I even went seven days in a row a couple times. There is a "seven" I managed to not "almost"...

I feel like this is becoming discouraging or self-deprecating. Maybe you just caught me on a bad day. Eventually, when I figure all of this out, I am going to write a book to all the Millennials who just can't seem to get it together. We'll finally find our place in this strange, broken world, hold hands around a bonfire at Dockweiler, and sing all the songs and poems we wrote about the struggles of this early century. Then we'll burn the lyrics and paddle out for a nice, easy-going surf at my favorite break, laughing as the sun sets over another perfect West Coast day. Until then, maybe you can find some solace in reading the rantings of a fellow member of this lost generation, finding that you are not alone in your shortcomings, hoping for better days and better waves.

THE LONG RIDE IN

ONE DAY I WANT to know how many hours I have spent waiting for the last wave of a surf session. You know what I mean: it's about time to go, but you want to end on a good one. Maybe your previous ride puttered out or you slipped on your board – there's no way you can go home on such a note. "One more ride," you say to yourself as you look out towards the horizon expectantly. Suddenly the lull between sets goes from fifteen minutes to about forty-five. The sun burns your head as you wait, having not reapplied sunscreen since you were going to leave anyway, bobbing up and down as the weak prospects of waves taunt you like your seventh grade crush dancing with her "boyfriend" from across the cafeteria to a Backstreet Boys love song while you pretend to not care about middle school dances (can you tell I speak from experience?).

Eventually, you either give up and ride the next whatever-it-is in back to the beach – after all, you have responsibilities to tend to. Of course, whenever this happens, usually a giant set rolls through right as you hit the sand. Your other option is to keep waiting…

and waiting...and waiting. Your friends that threw in the towel are also waiting on the beach, but not for waves; they are bone dry and wondering what it is you're hoping for – the swell is over, the tide is out and the sun is going down, after all.

Classic last-ride-in maneuver. (Photo by Justin Nanfelt)

However, sometimes this last ride is the most fun. You've had your session, gotten your rides, and now it's time to goof off on a party wave, gladiator-fighting in the whitewater as far as it pushes you. Or maybe you just ride this one in on your stomach and it is almost as much fun as riding the face (almost). Spray in your face, the six-inch wave pushes you at what feels like sixty miles per hour, being this close to the surface of the water. Carve around a little until the fins hit the sand and you're done. Nice way to end the day.

Yes, the last ride of the day is iconic, but also a dilemma. Some-times glorious and other times humble failure. Oftentimes packed, others lonely. But one thing you can count on: there is always a last wave, so make the most of it! You never know when your last wave will be your *last* wave, if you know what I mean.

"Teach us to number our days, that we may gain a heart of wisdom." *(Psalm 90:12)*

"Be very careful, then, how you live—not as unwise but as wise, making the most of every opportunity, because the days are evil. There- fore do not be foolish, but understand what the LORD's will is. Do not get drunk on wine, which leads to debauchery. Instead, be filled with the Spirit, speaking to one another with psalms, hymns, and songs from the Spirit. Sing and make music from your heart to the LORD, always giving thanks to God the Father for everything, in the name of our LORD Jesus Christ. Submit to one another out of reverence for Christ." (Ephesians 5:15-21)

If you've made it this far, it is no secret that this book has some re- ligious overtones (or should they be *undertows*? Get it?! Bad joke...) I thought maybe this would be a good point to reference where all of that started for me, especially given my somewhat ominous comments in the last piece...

I grew up going to church about half of the time (the other half we went to the beach, so you can see how writing this book came naturally to me). I didn't really like church or feel that comfortable there, however, mostly because I wasn't great at making friends when I was a child. Still, I had a deep sense of conviction about right and wrong, and knew that I needed to "ask Jesus into my heart" in order to go to Heaven, so that's what I did. A couple times actually, just to make sure I did it right.

I also feel the need to point out that my grandmother on my Dad's side (Granny) was a big religious influence on me, gifting us Christian things and teaching us Bible lessons whenever we stayed with her. I remember one Saturday morning we were watching some cartoon version of Bible stories and the sun was shining through the only window in her dusty apartment. It shone rays directly on the TV, which to me was a sign that God was approving of the programming. I shouted with excitement to tell Granny which she acknowledged in that nice grandmother sort of way. Anyway, in hindsight, she probably prayed for my sister and I a lot, because so much of my life and my spiritual journey doesn't really make sense, which means someone must have been looking out for me.

Fast-forward several years to my middle school years, where my preteen angst was at an all-time high. My main goal in life was to become a popular kid, something that had evaded me thus far. In the process of seeking this goal, I totally ditched my nerdy friends (who were mostly Christians), not being mean to them or anything like might happen in movies, but just spending a lot less time with them. My grades also tanked as I tried hard to be funny and accepted, instead of studying, apparently.

I'm probably unnecessarily proud to admit that I did, in fact, make it to a low-ish level of popularity, having been invited to a couple popular-kid parties and some other events. But by the end of my eighth-grade year, I could tell it just didn't fit me. I didn't really belong with them, and so I humbly went back to my old friends who welcomed me without hesitation.

I mention all of that middle school drama because it was something of a low point in my life and set the stage for what happened next. Throughout all of those formative years, I somehow found a deep love for Christian punk and ska music, and so when my friends Eric and Heath mentioned that their church was going to a Christian music festival the following summer, and that my favorite band, Five Iron Frenzy, was playing it, I knew I had to go.

I saved up, was gifted a little cash, and made the plans. Eventually, the long-awaited day came in the summer of 2000 when we boarded the 18-passenger van for the long ride up to Agape Farm in Shirleysburg, Pennsylvania. I had never experienced such a trip: hanging with good friends, making new ones, listening to great music on the way along with not a few fast food stops. We camped at the festival, exploring the mountain and a creek nearby. They had an amazing CD shop set up which had rare albums from punk bands I loved, as well as an on-site convenience store with the best chocolate milk I've ever tasted (those Pennsylvania Dutch really know how to milk a cow...and put lots of sugar in it). It was magical before it even really started, but that's when the life-change really happened.

If you have never been to an event like this, they usually have multiple stages, though everything culminates in the biggest bands of the festival each night, who perform after a good worship band set and some sort of speaker/sermon. I don't remember who the speaker was that night, but at the end of his talk he gave a choice to receive Jesus publicly, marking a decision to follow Him with intention and determination. Something about what he said felt like it was a decision I needed to make and so, when he asked those who wanted to accept the free gift of salvation from God, I stood up and made my way to the front of the stage to mark the moment, as well as receive a little "starter kit" for how to begin your relationship with God.

Now I think those little prayers I made in my room to allow Jesus in my heart as a child were significant, but something about this public decision seemed to provide a permanence to what I was saying. I write this because, ever since that day, my life really hasn't been the same. When I got home I started reading the Bible with a hunger I had never felt before. Everything in my life suddenly was seen through a spiritual lens. It brought a purpose to what I did, my everyday life at school, skateboarding, and the music I started to write (I had gotten a guitar about this same time).

My friend and fellow bandmate Heath helped get me to Creation, as well as bought me this sweet FIF shirt. (Photo by Heath Richardson)

Church was more fun and I started volunteering on the youth band a couple of years later, which *totally* changed my outlook on the institution. Wednesday nights became my favorite night of the week because I got to hang with other believers and play music that I also believed in. My little sister also started playing in the band and we became closer than we had ever been (we even liked some of the same music, though she gravitated towards heavier stuff, if you can believe it).

So there is my story. It's been over twenty years since that decision at Creation Festival and my life is still driven by a desire to know God and share that with others. I hope that this little testimony, as well as the stories in this book, inspire you in your own pursuit of God. He is certainly worth knowing, and I can say with a couple of decades of experience that, the deeper I go with Him, the more I land on this truth: "*God is love.*" *(1 John 4:8b)*

TAR ON MY BOARD

IT HAS BEEN HALF of a year since we left Los Angeles and there is still tar on my board from California. I'm not sure which break it came from, but it was likely Dockweiler. That place just oozes tar right out of the ground...literally. I've heard that tar comes up from under the ocean and makes its way to the beach, where it stains the sand black and sticks on unsuspecting surfers' feet. I remember walking up to the beach one day with my buddy Aaron and finding an almost completely black shore. The air smelled of oil, which doesn't make one want to paddle into the ocean very much. A big storm had come through offshore and blew all that junk inland, we figured. Maybe all those oilrigs that scar the skyline along the coast aren't worth it after all...

I noticed the tar on my second trip in the water here in Charleston. Yes, that is six months of living here and only two surf trips, if you're counting. I knew the waves were bad here, but I didn't expect them to be *that* bad. The busyness of getting settled, along with one-to-two-foot surf reports had kept me out of the water all summer.

Meanwhile, Russell told me he got the best waves of his life about two weeks after I left. "Double overhead, barreling as I stood straight up on a backside drop." My palm slapped my face as I wondered why we left in the first place.

They say, "The grass is always greener" when you're thinking that something (or somewhere) else is better than your current situation. During my seven years in Los Angeles, I fell a heavy victim to the Always Greener syndrome. There was always someplace better, somewhere closer to home with more family around or a slower pace of life – the big city just wasn't for me. Most of those places were literally greener, which was a big complaint during my tenure out West. It is a desert after all, so what did I expect?

Well, now I am back East, back *home*, and I am wishing for California surf – the mountains jutted right up to the beach, friends to ride with, and Jack in the Box to grab a nasty burger at on the way home from a Malibu surf session. It's got me second-guessing the whole move, why we're here, if God was in it or if we just made a colossal mistake.

This second trip out in the water was a choppy mess. I just wanted to surf really badly, and so I spent forty-five minutes driving to the beach for a twenty-minute session. The great thing about the southeast is that the water gets warm in the summer – I mean bath-water warm – but as I stepped into the Atlantic for that quick session on a Monday morning, I noticed the water was much colder than I remembered. Maybe it's because of climate change and I'm just swimming in the remnants of an unfortunate iceberg that drifted too far beyond the Arctic Circle; or maybe I am just looking for reasons to be negative. My first thought as that slight chill hit my mildly tan legs was, "Great, the water's cold here too. The only *good* thing about surfing the East Coast is gone now." One more reason to have stayed in California I figured...

As I drove home from an uneventful surf at the Washout, save a couple rides and some fun wipeouts, I felt the grimy fingers of comparison gripping their slippery claws around me. It's been a non-stop battle these past months, with doubt and discontentment ripping me to pieces. But when I noticed the tar on my surfboard I remembered that California has its flaws too. The cold water is a pain and I don't like wearing wetsuits. The beaches are more crowded. Traffic is terrible. It's cloudy in the summer. The summers are also flat. The sharks are big. And there's tar in the water.

Even Dockweiler has airplanes taking off overhead that interrupt your conversations, which are hard enough to hear between breaking waves and Mitchel's mumbly New Zealand/Australian anomaly of an accent. When I was there, I spent my time in between sets shivering and dreaming of warmer waters. Now I sit in warmer waters dreaming of bigger waves. "The human heart is never happy," someone once told me, and I guess it is true.

But in the midst of all that negativity (don't worry, I won't end the book on a downer), I have a decision to make: Will I constantly compare where I am at to where I am not, or will I enjoy the moment I am in? Will I always look to the past as a better time and not acknowledge the good that is happening now (the "Killer Nostalgia" as I like to call it)? Will I continually plan for the future, expecting the next time and place to be better than the current? Or will I simply exist in this moment; enjoying the time I am given, because I am certainly not guaranteed another breath?

"But Godliness with contentment is great gain. For we brought nothing into the world, and we can take nothing out of it." (1 Timothy 6:6-7)

Though my heart longs for California, I cannot step into past circumstances, nor can I be there now. To wish I were is to neglect the gift of the present that I have been entrusted with. Maybe we'll go back, or maybe we won't. I hope to visit and surf the sunny beaches of the Golden Coast many more times, but as for now I'll have to seek the beauty of the Lowcountry, with its muddy waters and hollow waves. The sun still shimmers on these waters and the salt still stings; like whiskey around your tongue, it intoxicates as it draws you in. The waves peel a dull brown against the hazy blue sky, humidity filling your lungs with water, with life, as you paddle into the soft rising sun over the horizon. There is beauty here. It's up to you and me to find it.

Maybe all roads lead to Dockweiler, or maybe they stop here at Folly Road. Either way, I hope *your* road leads you to an ocean, where the majestic power of a simple thing like energy plowing through water can hold your gaze, take your breath, fill your ears, and sting your senses all at the same time; beckoning you out into something bigger than yourself and leading you to adventures you could never find on dry land. To places where you can learn lessons about contentment, fear, and humility; where memories are cemented and friendships are crafted. Moments where you see something beyond our day-to-day lives, examine your place in this big world, and hopefully meet the God who created it all out on the water, where I did, and continue to do so, as often as I can.

> *"Though the fig tree does not bud*
> *and there are no grapes on the vines, though the olive crop fails*
> *and the fields produce no food, though there are no sheep in the pen*
> *and no cattle in the stalls, yet I will rejoice in the Lord,*
> *I will be joyful in God my Savior.*
> *The Sovereign Lord is my strength; He makes my feet like the feet*
>   *of a deer,*
> *He enables me to tread on the heights." (Habakkuk 3:17-19)*

"But he said to me, 'My grace is sufficient for you, for my power is made perfect in weakness.' Therefore I will boast all the more gladly about my weaknesses, so that Christ's power may rest on me. That is why, for Christ's sake, I delight in weaknesses, in insults, in hardships, in persecutions, in difficulties. For when I am weak, then I am strong." (2 Corinthians 12:9-10)

EPILOGUE

CONTENTMENT

FEELS LIKE CALIFORNIA

TOWARDS THE END OF my tenure in Los Angeles I got into property management, more out of necessity than preference. Still, it allowed me to work from home and watch our newborn daughter, while also placing us a mere two miles from the beach. I had a handful of on-call babysitters, so when I had a work meeting (or a big swell was coming through), I could call them up for a few hours and get done what I needed to. (A big thanks goes out to Uncle Randy, Jen, Chelsea, and Michelle for that, by the way.)

When we made the move back east, the first job I could land was as an Assistant Manager at a much larger property in Mt. Pleasant, SC. Mt. Pleasant really is a magical place. Growing up, it was clean, quaint, and had this air of possibility that was only magnified at its nearest beach, the Isle of Palms. So, when I started working there at a property only four miles from the beach, I naturally had to go for a before- or after-work surf session. These types of things tend to elude me though (I once worked an entire year in Huntington Beach – aka "Surf City" – and didn't surf a single day), and so it was about four months before I managed to paddle out.

By the time 5:00PM flashed on the time clock, I was out the door. I almost didn't go to the beach because the sun was going down quickly in the mid-fall season. It had been a long time since I surfed though, and so I owed it to myself to at least try. As I drove over the tall bridge that crosses the Intracoastal Waterway onto IOP, I saw an amazing sunset to my right. The big red ball looked especially huge on this crisp October evening, making it difficult to imagine something that large traversing the sky, making its way across the wide United States to the Pacific coast I still longed for (I know that's not how the Sun works, scientifically, but let me wax poetic for a moment here…).

In fact, by the time I found a (free) parking space and put my wetsuit on, it was almost too late to surf, but I was also too far to turn back. The air was misty and cool, the wind blowing and the water choppy. Really, it was a terrible day to surf, with two-to-three-foot waves amongst a plethora of wind chop. I ran to a spot by the pier where a couple of locals were fishing. I imagined they thought I was a little crazy paddling out so near to nighttime into a mess of waves by myself. Sharks tend to eat at sunset and fishermen attract sharks, but again, I was too far gone to turn back.

As I watched the fishermen watch me, it struck me that I was still very much the same surfer that I was on the West Coast. Still spooked by sharks (probably needlessly), still making the most of tiny surf (now absolutely necessary) and of course, still wasting time finding free parking when I could be surfing (maybe I should learn to let this one go…). A surfer is a surfer, I suppose, no matter his location.

The session was awful. I actually didn't paddle out to the proper break because of fear, and just rode a couple little beach breakers the best I could. It all kind of felt like a waste of time, really, but I had to do it. The months leading up to this of little-to-no surfing were amongst the worst of my life, not just because of the surfing, though it certainly played a part. As you know, before I moved to California I was a casual surfer, with three to five sessions a year usually sufficing my need to be in the water. I even classified it as my third favorite sport, with skateboarding and snowboarding taking the top spots. (I'm big on having favorite lists – ask me for my list of bands and movies some time.) As this book describes, I came to fall in love with the sport. It captured me in a place I did not know was there and prompted a journey I did not expect. I usually tell people who are interested in surfing that there are two responses after the first time you go: you can either take it or leave it, or it grips your heart and you have to surf over and over again for the rest of your life. Somehow I made a progression from the first to the second, so I guess I can relate to everyone now.

The problem with all of it is I didn't know how far gone I was. I sincerely thought I was ready to leave the West Coast, surfing and all, and make a life somewhere east. I knew the waves would be worse, but maybe a standup paddleboard or the occasional weekend trip to the Outer Banks would suffice. However, like the roots of the palm trees that so famously mark the city I lived in, the roots of surfing went deeper than the eye suggests.

After about two waves, the sun was down pretty far and I decided I had had enough. On the way back I saw a ghost crab and was reminded of my wife's family vacations in North Carolina, where we once took flashlights to go spotting for the elusive scuttlers. I was lucky enough to experience two of those weeks with her large family, and even luckier to surf nearly every day of both trips. But even the waves on those days were spotty and mostly smallish. It is a beautiful place, but the thought of it all brought me to a decision: I must return to California.

The strand at IOP on this mild October evening. (Photo by Author)

The strand at the Isle of Palms reminded me of Hermosa Beach, where I used to catch the occasional crappy beach break. In Hermosa, there are coffee shops and an excellent Mexican restaurant where my wife and I would take our daughter, often watching the sunset after dinner. There were playgrounds on the beach and even an outdoor amphitheater where we *almost* saw Jimmy Buffett play one time! (For free, at that...)

The air was sweet that evening, reminding me of my years spent taking in cool Charleston evenings, particularly in the summer. I had to ask myself: is that smell unique to Charleston, where the thick damp humidity collides with the cool of the evening, the ocean salt mixing with the sweet aroma of pralines cooking downtown? Maybe so, but it smelled a lot like spring in California, where the bougainvillea bloom and the windy Pacific air wafts through the City of Angels. I never loved spring in the South because of the humidity, but in California, it became one of my favorite seasons.

Even though my ears and nose were full of water, a different ocean but salty nonetheless, from a few too many thrashings on not a few too closed-out waves. Really, the whole thing kind of felt like California, and so I had to ask myself another question: Was I just being unappreciative? Much of the country doesn't even live by the coast and here I was being picky about *which* coast I enjoyed. Attitude is everything, so maybe I have just been ungrateful for the gifts given me.

But then the air was misty like the West Coast, the June Gloom that stretches across so many of the spots I found familiar during the spring and summer months. A helicopter flew overhead, much like the constant noise of big city life with its weather and police helicopters showing up at all hours of the night. I even hit traffic on the way home, unexpected at such an hour. Have I found the California of the East Coast? Is it all really more or less the same beach life?

Or is the Pacific calling my name?

Calling me home…

SOUTHERN SONG (I MUST GO)

There's a song about the South in me
But I'm having trouble finding it
The words swirl round my tongue
But I can't seem to rhyme with them
When I look into my heart
It's not the whole but just the part
Chase the sun out to the West
To find the rest

When I smell the evening air here
And the salty sea shines black
Southern winds blow through my hair
And I am instantly brought back
My sullen heart begins to swell
At days of old, forgotten tales
Watch the sun rise in the East
On homely seas

A compass rose ain't a guide
It just points you everywhere
And your heart will seldom tell a lie
When it's splayed out open, bare
And can you ever find a home
Without leaving yours to roam?
I don't think so, and that's why I must go

A compass rose ain't a guide
It just points you everywhere
And your broken heart will seldom lie
When it's splayed out open, bare
And can you ever find a home
Without leaving yours to roam?
I don't think so, and that's why I must go

The horizon's calling this Southern son
Seeking solace over sands and snow
I still love you, and I'm sorry but I must go

WRONG LANE

HAVE YOU EVER BEEN stuck in traffic, and every lane seems to be going faster than yours? When you finally make the last-ditch move to get over, *that* lane suddenly slows down, as if it was only waiting for you, like you are the reason everyone is going slow in the first place. I thought I was crazy in thinking this way, but then I heard a pastor confirm the same suspicions, so I know I am at least supported...

This of course happens all the time in Los Angeles, particularly on the 405-freeway, which is a massive multi-lane highway that, as the book title suggests, leads to Dockweiler (with that short exit to the 105, of course). I was thinking about this yesterday because in this year of being stripped down to nothing, with not even surfing as a comfort, I am realizing that maybe I was in the wrong lane all these years.

As I wrote before, I have spent a lot of time wishing I was somewhere else, and this year was possibly the culmination of it all. I was wanting so badly to be back in California with its cool breeze and bigger waves, and day-dreaming about those things just about every day while in the South. I am learning though, that this is all folly. Existing in any moment besides the one you are in is a waste of time, and as I conclude this journey, I must surmise that this is the result of my experience. It has come in little bits and waves, but here at the one-year-since mark, I am finding fresh epiphanies concerning the topic; ones that will hopefully settle into convictions and life change.

An example: I have been listening to a lot of The Head and the Heart this year, partly because they came out with a new, very Los Angeles/big city-sounding album; but also because the band reminds me of LA. This album (no longer "new," but new when I wrote this) even has a song called "City of Angels," for crying out loud, all about the songwriter's love for the town. But when I reminisce about listening to the music in said city, it is funny what two very vivid memories often float to the top. The first is reasonable: my early morning drive to El Porto for the Trishredathon surf session, when the air was cool and the sky a crisp blue, shattered only by the breaking of a beautiful rising sun. But the second is surprising: sitting in traffic on La Cienega after work.

My favorite album of theirs came out when I had an eight-to-five job (whatever happened to nine-to-five anyway?) at NBCUniversal, about eleven miles away from home. Well, eleven miles in rush hour traffic might was well be sixty miles, because it's going to take at least an hour. But somehow I look fondly on that drive, specifically a day when I was heading south and the sun was setting to my right, coloring the sky a beautiful ombré hue. I don't know why this was significant, but I remember the day with a smile, my long commute home after a boring day in the office.

And so, this memory leads to me to a conclusion or two. First, no matter what your circumstances, there is something about your current situation that you will one day look back on with a fond smile. Second, that smile may come out of some crappy situations!

As I think back on my time in LA, I remember moving with four other roommates into a two-bedroom apartment, no job, and just enough money saved up to last a few months. This led to countless nights of bonding with friends, watching *The O.C.*, and hanging out at the Grove. I also remember getting bed bugs and a tumultuous six-month period in our lives when we trashed most of our furniture and lost our status as the "cool apartment," where people once chose to hang out, but now avoided us like we had a plague.

I think about interning at companies, working for free but making lifelong friends. I remember finally landing a "solid" full-time job, but ending up on the night shift for a year, which will do things to your brain that you don't want done and leave you too tired to think about it afterwards. I had to move out of my apartment (then six people in a two-bedroom) because the new addition was an opera singer who needed to practice while I was trying to sleep because of my night shift.

I remember "family dinners" with those same roommates, where we ate at the ugly, orange, never-finished table my good friend Ben and I built, drinking "two-buck chuck" (cheap wine from Trader Joe's) with orange juice. These folks truly were our family, the bed bug incident having solidified a bond that few things really can. They are the same friends who helped me propose to my wife and throw the best party we ever threw (outside of our wedding), where literally every person danced, even those who historically "don't dance." (Our love will make the world dance, baby!)

Of course these were the years where I fell in love with surfing, but then moved to Highland Park, closer to my wife's work. This was an awesome area of LA to explore, with great skateparks, but far away from the beach and most of our friends. Next was the year we moved to Westchester, the closest to the beach that either of us had ever lived. That was the summer where I surfed more than I ever have, and also when we found out we were pregnant, causing us to leave the little slice of heaven that we had discovered.

After that we spent two years in Redondo Beach, then a whopping two miles from the beach, with a new area to explore. It was a change of careers for me, combined with learning how to be a dad, both of which brought joy and pain in various ways. Distance from friends and family made this season difficult, though I almost daily reminisce about the South Bay and all its hidden treasures.

Really, this chapter could be much, much longer as I think about the ups and downs of our time in Los Angeles. But through the good and bad I have to remember that, as The Head and the Heart sings, "There will always be better days." And the seed of those better days is planted in momentary contentment, continually renewed as we try not to forget all that we have been given.

I was afraid of ending this book on a concession: "Oh well, maybe I'll go back and score some waves another day…" That's no way to end something and it's not how my story is going. I am learning a far greater lesson than how to surf ten-foot walls in Southern California. I am learning how to be happy anywhere, waves or no waves. It is still a process, and I am certainly not there yet, but I think that this is the story of those years, and the story of this book. In a way, it's like Dockweiler beach: truthfully, it's kind of a crappy break. There are a lot better places to surf, but for me, it's my favorite. I'm content there.

And you should be too.

"I am not saying this because I am in need, for I have learned to be content whatever the circumstances. I know what it is to be in need, and I know what it is to have plenty. I have learned the secret of being

content in any and every situation, whether well fed or hungry, whether living in plenty or in want. I can do all this through Him who gives me strength." (Philippians 4:11-13)

AFTERWORD
BOOKENDS

THE RETURN

IT HAD BEEN ONE year to the week since I had stepped foot on Pacific shores. I had never imagined I would go that long without that crunchy sand between my toes, but with crazy work schedules and family responsibilities, I really had no choice. Now the time came – my brother-in-law Randy was set to marry his sweetheart Rachel and we had a legitimate reason to travel to California outside of catching a good swell (which, of course, is a legitimate reason to me, though my bosses may have thought otherwise).

The flight was tumultuous; riding standby (for free, thanks to one of my jobs) is no cakewalk. It began with a rushed traversal over five terminals in the busy Atlanta airport, only to find a closed door to Santa Ana, followed by a slightly less-rushed four-terminal run (I was tired), including a spill at the top of an escalator, luggage splayed out but only my ego damaged. I finally made it onto the LAX plane and immediately felt the California vibe surround me. Wide-brimmed hats and plenty of denim, along with that "too cool for school" attitude filled the plane as I settled in and tried to sleep. Russell picked me up and we headed for a late-night snack at Wurstküche in Downtown LA before crashing at his place. If I hadn't made that second plane (again, standby), no surf would have happened, and so I'm going to go ahead and say that God divinely sent me back so I could have a good ending for this book. (That's sound doctrine, right?)

The next morning we got up and considered a Point Dume run. It would have taken an hour-and-a-half in rush hour traffic though, and I had to be in Palm Springs by mid-afternoon for wedding festivities. So we headed to the familiar South Bay, catching a little bit of the southwest swell LA was getting (though not as much as Dume was unfortunately). I coaxed Russell into checking out Dockweiler, just in case it looked good, but mostly because of nostalgia.

The break was just as I remembered it. A couple guys aimlessly paddled around, but overall it was flat. Still, the sight of familiar lifeguard tower forty-nine, the jetty, the park, the palms; everything about the place caused a joy to leap inside me I had rarely felt on the East Coast.

This was home, and I was finally back.

Dockweiler during the return. (Photo by Author)

Nostalgia aside, surfers will chase waves despite our emotions (especially Russell), and so we drove south to Hammerland to find a mostly empty break. Parking was only $3, which is less than I remembered it. The long walk to the beach was pleasant as I watched the bike riders and runners with envy: *They* live *here*, I thought, *just like I used to*. For them, this was routine, as it once was for me. The air was warm, but not too hot. No humidity. The sun shone brightly as it slowly rose. The water was a glassy blue as tiny surf broke on the dirty sand. As far as I was concerned, I was back in paradise.

We paddled out to the north side of the jetty at Hammerland, seeing some corners on left-breaking waves. Russell made a comment about how he said left, when in actuality we were on the right side of the jetty. "Surfer's left," I called it, realizing we were on the same page without even knowing it. Sometimes surfing just binds people together, you know?

The water was colder than I expected, though not too bad. It was May after all. Thankfully Russell had a spare 4/3, along with a spare Al Merrick "Neck Beard" – it's good to have friends who are overly invested in surfing. Unfortunately, the Neck Beard is a little squirrelier than the ...*Lost* I had been riding the past year, and so on my first several waves, I had a bad stance and just jostled about at the base of the wave until it crashed prematurely on me. Nonetheless, despite bad rides, I was beside myself with happiness. The magic of the Pacific was once again in my life and it felt unreasonably good. More than that, I was struck by how natural everything was. It felt as though I had never left, as if this is just what we do: Go surf Hammerland mid-week while all the suckers are at work, maybe hit a taco stand on the way home, and then go back to being semi-responsible.

No surprise, things in LA had gone relatively unchanged. The smoke stacks were still marking the spot like an ugly reminder of man's progression butting against nature's beauty. Oil rigs and giant ships stacked high with containers marked the shoreline, perhaps a few more than I remembered. I could still see Palos Verdes to the south and Santa Monica to the north, Malibu jutting out just past that, visible because the day was clear. I really felt like I was home, and had just been away on a long vacation, or a long work trip.

I only caught a handful of waves, most of them weak because I was not used to the board. I was worried that my skills as a surfer would have faded tremendously after a year of hardly riding. Russell had claimed that this past winter was the best he had ever surfed, which made me worry that he would have surpassed me and we would no longer be compatible surf partners. Not that he would ever deny a friend a surf, but you know what I mean… I was pleased to find, though, that I paddled out fine and caught the waves given me. A few slips spoiled my rides, but that's normal – after all, I wasn't a great surfer a year ago so there was no reason I should shred a year later.

Russell found a little boyle that would kick you up into a wave right next to the jetty. He got a great left from that, but both of us had trouble duplicating the ride. My best one was a strange right I almost didn't go for. It looked like it would just roll over me, but Russell offered a quick, "Here you go," and so I paddled. It's strange how the suggestion of a second opinion will lead us to action, despite the doubts in our own heads. I paddled and caught what turned into a long right that seemed out of place. Other than that, I got a nice left later on and then paddled in because the cold water had cramped my legs up, which is usually my signal that it is time to quit.

I mentioned many pages ago a feeling you get when you are in decent-sized waves and, as you gaze out to the horizon for the next set, a standout approaches, way past where you are. Fear leaps within you as you paddle like a fiend to beat the break, or maybe catch it if you get lucky. I often tell people that I inexplicably miss that feeling – being afraid and excited at the same time. It is like a test of skill, of timing, of knowing the ocean and surviving the punches it throws. It is a feeling I hadn't really felt in a year of surfing Charleston, but I am happy to write that I had it that day at Hammerland. A strange standout set of about eight waves busted in after a long lull, and as I paddled towards the beginning of it, I was reminded of what it was like to approach waves that scared you. They weren't that big, so the feeling wasn't too strong, but they had a little power and a little size, which was enough to remind me of my humble place in this great ocean.

Russell had taken to calling these rare waves "Prayer Waves." This started a little over a year prior when he, Dan, and I were surfing this same spot. I kept catching waves but they kept missing. "Maybe we need to get saved, Rick," Russell quipped.

"Saved from what?" I asked, trying to be clever. I knew what he was talking about though. Early on in our friendship he asked if I was a Christian. "Yeah, but not in the way you think," I said, trying to distance myself from stereotypes of judgmental, legalistic Christians. He is an atheist (though sometimes more agnostic), with many very intelligent opinions about the subject. Over the years we have had great conversations on faith, all without a hint of anger or animosity. This type of relationship is one of my favorite things about surfing – the mutual respect between us allowed us to differ in opinion about a major aspect of our lives, one that we spoke about often thanks to the long drives to and from Malibu with not a few fast food visits during transit.

Surfing lends itself well to good conversations and shared opinions along with shared stoke. Surfers are typically humble and also willing to talk about the deeper things in life. There are a whole host of reasons for this, one of the biggest being a constant reminder of our lowly place in this world, thanks to the guaranteed thrashing we receive from the heavy oceans we surf. What a beautiful thing it is to paddle out together with brothers into a battle bigger than us.

Anyway, that was just the initial seed of the Prayer Wave. About a month prior to my visit I called Russell, and he immediately asked, "Did Dan tell you to call me?"

"No," I replied. Russell explained that he had just gotten off the phone with Dan, complaining about a whole host of LA drama that was going on in his life. He had mentioned that maybe he needed to ask me for prayer, after which I "coincidentally" happened to call. There are no coincidences, my friends; everything happens for a reason.

During that phone call, he told me about how he had paddled out at Malibu about month before that. We had spoken that day and he told me to send some prayer waves his way. He was going through the same drama, but was surfing as a little escape. It turns out that the waves were pretty flat and he was sitting far out, waiting for a standout to come (as he often does). I believe he said he had a feeling a wave would show up, and so he paddled somewhere else. Suddenly, out of nowhere, an exceptional right popped up and he was in perfect position. He rode that wave to glory and, from that moment on, referred to it as the Prayer Wave. I was honored to have sent it and hoped that the experience boosted my good friend's faith.

And so that was the big return. We surfed for about an hour and then went back, where I had a quick lunch with my sister Nicky and then made the drive to Palm Springs for a beautiful wedding. The whole thing made me wonder why I ever left. Even the desert had perfect weather that weekend, including a memorable afternoon with my kids on heavily irrigated and therefore lush green grass complete with that cool California breeze I so missed. On the way back to the airport, we got lucky and happened across a luncheon some friends were having for two child dedications at our old church, Ecclesia in Hollywood. Most of our good friends in LA were attending, and so we crashed the party. Again, it all just felt like home, like we had never left.

But the truth of the matter is that LA is not home anymore, and to wish it was only perpetuates an unmet longing that will inevitably lead to discontent. At the lunch party I met a guy named Nate. He had had a similar experience to me – living and working in Los Angeles for several years and eventually returning home for cheaper housing and to be closer to family. He said that every time he came back to LA he had to check himself and those feelings of longing, asking questions about where they came from and whether or not they were from God. Eventually they got weaker and weaker, much the same way my longings for Charleston got weaker the longer I was in Los Angeles after my initial move. You see, I spent several years in LA wishing for the green East Coast, and now that I was back, I was wishing for the West. That kind of mentality is lose-lose, for obvious reasons.

When we got back east, I had a long talk with my wife about happiness and contentment, still reluctant to let go of California. And then, that same week I had another similar talk with a lady at work that I hardly knew, who immediately told me the same thing. When you get that many seemingly unconnected voices in your life saying the same thing, eventually you have to give in. And I guess that's what this is all about – letting go.

I have had the most fun writing this book; more than anything else I have ever written. Reminiscing is one of my favorite things to do, but, as I've said before, nostalgia can be a killer. C.S. Lewis wrote in *The Screwtape Letters* that the best places to meet God are in the faraway past, the present, and the faraway future. The past in remembering what He has done, the present because that is the only moment we have, and the future in looking forward to Heaven. Existing in my mind in those nearly seven years in Los Angeles is nowhere on that spectrum, and so I guess it has to stop. Or at least it must pale in comparison to my enjoyment of the present moment, wherever I am at and whatever size the waves are.

And so to you, Reader, I charge the same action: enjoy the moment you are in for what it is, because we are not guaranteed another. Maybe you are in Malibu now, reading this book to learn about Los Angeles and its waves; or maybe you're in Maryland wishing for sunny days and sparkling Pacific waters. Whatever the case, decide to be happy now, and let nothing hinder that. Let go of the past, look forward to the future, but no matter what, enjoy the moment you're in. Life is too short not to.

"…one thing I do: Forgetting what is behind and straining toward what is ahead, I press on toward the goal to win the prize for which God has called me heavenward in Christ Jesus. All of us, then, who are mature should take such a view of things." (Philippians 3:13b-15a)

THE DEATH OF DOCKWEILER

SOMETIMES IN LIFE YOU have to choose to let something go, and sometimes you are forced to. Your hand is laid out before you and folding is your only option. Last week I got a call from Mitchel with some bad news about my beloved break and my struggle with contentment was given one such death blow...

It seems there were some political problems concerning the parking at Dockweiler. It has always been an issue of sorts, with folks parking in all sorts of strange places to get their coveted beach days along with about a thousand other Angelino beach-goers. The scene became dangerous as bystanders were crossing the four-lane road while inconsiderate LA drivers were speeding along their way, blatantly ignoring the beauty that was before them (as well as some pedestrians). The solution was to crack down on parking and install some yellow plastic poles in the center, as well as about a hundred "No U-turn" signs, forcing drivers looking for parking to get far away from the fire pits before turning around to try again. This happened while I lived there, and worked well enough for the time, but I suppose more recently the powers that be decided to eliminate two of the four lanes, and put in diagonal parking, something Hermosa did on the aforementioned Herondo Street. The solution favored surfers and beach-goers alike, though commuters were finding that traffic was building, and in a city like Los Angeles, more traffic might as well be like more cancer.

And so the politicians and city planners (and I would argue, the rich Silicon Beach landowners) dealt a blow to the beach that I love (without even consulting me, the nerve…), and eliminated street parking altogether. ALL OF IT, save about eight spots on the non-beach side of the street, adjacent to a little playground where kids seldom play but airline workers take their breaks. Now you have to get lucky enough to snag one of those spots or pay to park in the state beach lot down the hill, which Mitchel mentioned had been lowered to a modest $3 during weekdays (they've since raised it).

Now you may be reading this and thinking, *Rick is over-reacting. Parking does not mean the* death *of Dockweiler.* Maybe so. But when I told my wife, she concurred – this is a fatal blow. You see, one of the things that was so magical about Dockweiler is that you had a choice to risk unloading your car while traffic sped by before stumbling down the sandy hill with said luggage, sometimes three-or-more times per outing, or pay $10 and park near the beach. Something about that choice to save money and replace it with danger just oozes charisma, as well as deeply identifies with one of the pillars of my personality. Sure, Dockweiler isn't dead, but Dockweiler as I *knew it* is, and that is what I am writing about.

It has been over a year and I am still struggling with losing Los Angeles. I have made headway, and the previous few chapters have been evidence of it, but something still feels off, even as I re-read the truthful claims that I have made so strongly. I miss LA, for a lot of reasons, one of the biggest being the surf. Not just surfing itself, but what this book is about: the surf adventures and the friends that have joined me along the way. The feelings aren't as strong as they used to be, but they are still there. I am learning to be happy where I am at, but if I am honest, a big part of me still longs to be on the West Coast.

I was at work the other day and had some time to kill. Lucky for me, one of the most beautiful sunsets was happening right then, so I sat and watched it. First I would like to say, it has become difficult in this present age to simply *watch* a sunset. Phones and productivity are so distracting that I literally had to decide to enjoy this moment rather than take a picture and move on to something else. It is sad that the world in which we live is so fast-paced that a simple sunset is hardly worth a pause. I watched as a coworker exited the building, whipped out his phone and snapped a few pics before heading back inside, barely using his own eyes to take a glance at the beauty before him. I cannot hold it against him too badly though, for it took a hefty resolve to not do the same thing myself.

The second thing I noticed is that, even with this beauty before me, all I could think about was the plethora of sunsets I have watched at Dockweiler, and how I wanted to be there again. (I work at the airport in Charleston, and LAX is right on the other side of Dockweiler, making it not so difficult to imagine my favorite beach on the other side of Terminal B.) I longed for the beach days that climaxed in a glorious sunset over the Pacific, followed by a denouement of s'mores over a bonfire with friends while the desert chill set in. It consumed me, so much so that I almost couldn't enjoy what my own eyes were beholding at that moment.

But alas, the Dockweiler I once knew has been decimated, destroyed by worker-bees and their daily commutes. My struggle is lessened through necessity. I considered changing everything I wrote about the glory days in this book since they are not true anymore, but decided against it. This book is now, and shall forever be, a memorial to what once was. You can still surf Dockweiler, of course, but the freedom I once enjoyed is gone, maybe not forever, but maybe so. (I fully intend to send this book, along with a strongly worded letter, to the appropriate politicians, by the way.) And if that is the case, I want you and everyone else who dreams about the California life to know the cool evenings and hot afternoons of a mediocre Los Angeles beach break that has burrowed its way into my heart.

And there it remains: in my heart, and in the pages of this book, which I hope captures enough emotion to inspire you to go and find your own Dockweiler. There is a feeling that cannot be duplicated, and seldom even expressed adequately, that Dockweiler symbolizes for me. The waves, water, weather. Sea, swell, sounds. Fire, food, friends. Sunsets and surfing. Music and memories. It all ties together into something I want you to catch a glimpse of in these modest pages, and then experience for yourself. And so as you finish this last page, I hope you set it down with a smile, and then head out the door with a board under your arms. If not a board, a guitar, notebook and pencil, your child's hand. Seek the place that sets your heart on fire and sit there awhile, letting it ignite in you a flame that carries you through the mundane, until that flicker grows dim, and a return visit is required.

As for me, I will remain content to reminisce with an open hand, hoping for another session at the beach I love, but knowing that, should it never take place, greater things await me yet. A mountain, a beach, home, Heaven. For as long as the God who made the shore is my pursuit, I will never lack, and the journey will inevitably lead to a place even better than Dockweiler State Beach.

SING SONG

I woke up this morning
Ready to sing
A song in my mind
In my heart, there's a theme
And it's You...oh, You

There's a chill in the air
But it's warm enough to run
Through the trees and the beaches
Under the sun
With You...oh, with You

In our hearts, there's a song
You can try hard to keep it in
But you will find before too long
If you're walking close with Him
You can't help but sing...oh, sing.

I have a beautiful wife
And a pretty little girl
With another on the way
To brighten up my world
With You...because of You

I have a place to live
And a means to provide
With the mountains in the distance
And beaches right outside
With You...because of You

There's a blessing on the ridge
And another in the sea
And if we step in stride with Him
Through the storms in between
We can sing...oh, sing

Even when it's night
With the darkness all around
I'll keep my eyes on the stars
And an ear to the ground
For You...listening for You

And when the time is right
The sun will rise with warmth
For yonder breaks
A new and glorious morn
With You...another day with You!

ABOUT THE AUTHOR

RICK LIVES WITH HIS wife and two daughters in Los Angeles, CA (yes, they did eventually move back), where he still surfs, skates, and snowboards whenever he can. He is sponsored by Intrusive Skateboards and Soul Performance Surf and Skate Shop, and is only a little bit bitter that Wavestorm never offered him a spot on their team (though he hopes this book may change that!). A hopeless creative, he produces music under the publishing company Rootster Recordings, his most personal project being the alt-folk Yonder Breaks, while also writing books, screenplays, and shooting the occasional skate video in between. Basically, he does all the things he did back in high school, but now gets paid for it (sometimes). You can find out more about Rick and what he is up to by visiting www.YonderBreaks.com.